Moon City Review 2009

An Annual
of Poetry, Story, Art, & Criticism

Moon City Review 2009

An Annual
of Poetry, Story, Art, & Criticism

Edited by Jane Hoogestraat & Lanette Cadle
Missouri State University

Springfield, Missouri
2009

For inquiries contact:
Editor, Moon City Review
Department of English
Missouri State University
Springfield MO 65897
Email: MoonCityReview@missouristate.edu
Web: http://english.missouristate.edu/moon_city_review.htm

Cover Photography: "Sprinkler" (front cover) and "Bratz Dolls"
(back cover) by Julie Blackmon, copyright © 2009

Cover design: Lanette Cadle and Rebecca Sloane
Text layout: Angelia Northrip-Rivera

Library of Congress Cataloging-in-Publication Data

Moon city review 2009 : an annual of poetry, story, art, & criticism
/ edited by Jane Hoogestraat & Lanette Cadle.
      p. cm.
  ISBN 978-0-913785-20-1
   1. College students' writings, American--Missouri. 2. Missouri
State University--Literary collections. 3.   Missouri--Literary
collections. 4. American literature--Missouri. I. Hoogestraat, Jane
Susan, 1959- II. Cadle, Lanette. III. Moon city review.
  PS508.C6M58 2009
  810.8'006--dc22
                                        2009029569

Contents

II. Direct from Moon City

III. Archival Treasures from the Ozarks

Dedicated to Robert H. Henigan,

who started it all.

Welcome to Moon City

Jane Hoogestraat
with James S. Baumlin

Introduction and Acknowledgments

1. What We're About.

The following paragraphs present a manifesto of sorts, an explanation of what we're intending. In the fall of 1989, creative writing faculty at what was then Southwest Missouri State (and what is now Missouri State University) formed the Moon City Reading Series, aimed at showcasing the work of faculty, students, and members of the Springfield community. Over the last two decades, the Moon City Reading Series has continued uninterrupted and flourished; happily, we look forward to a formal celebration of its 20th anniversary. The university, the city of Springfield, and the English department's creative writing program have all grown, at times exponentially. *Moon City Review 2009: An Annual of Poetry, Story, Art, & Criticism* reflects the growth and maturity of this program.

With this present volume, *Moon City Review (MCR)* changes shape, moving from a predominantly student-run bi-annual journal (housed in the Missouri State University English Department) to a book annual featuring work in various genres from multiple communities: from current students and faculty to celebrated alums and artists of regional, national, even international reputation. In its cornucopian variety, its student/faculty/community collaborations, and its commitment to future "special, themed editions," *MCR* has become an unabashedly experimental, hybrid text, unique in scope and Quixotic—in the best sense—in its ambitions. In sum, *we wish to be read* and to be read widely, showing the world what we in Springfield, Missouri, can do and what our extended area and former Ozarkers can do. We wish to make *MCR* a home for the region's and nation's poets, fiction writers, story-tellers, artists, scholars, critics.

What ties these communities together for us is the *MCR* editors' belief that serious creative writers (and critical writers), at any level, are all apprenticed to the same practice of high quality writing. This apprenticeship model avoids any strictly hierarchical divisions, in which undergraduates theoretically form the bottom rung on a ladder whose top rung is occupied by Pulitzer Prize winners. For us in this volume and in the future, the measure will be the excellence of the work rather than the status of the writer. This first volume does that, intentionally placing undergraduate poets in the very fine company of Ted Kooser, Burton Raffel, and Miller Williams. And our student fiction writers find themselves in the similarly stellar company of John Dufresne, Michael Czyniejewski, and Kevin Brockmeier. Rather than the aforementioned (and rejected) hierarchical arrangement, we opted for an arrangement that presents a seamless community of writers and artists who will most likely find themselves among good company, indeed. All submissions were carefully peer-reviewed. Taken together, we believe our contributors offer a literary/artistic conversation of high and thought-provoking quality.

MCR has a mission to provide student writers as well as professionals with a venue for their work. Missouri State University offers a unique opportunity to its students as one of the few schools that allows undergraduate creative writing courses (in poetry, fiction, and creative nonfiction) to satisfy a "general education" requirement. We do so in the belief that exposure to the creative arts, including exposure to a range of literary aesthetics, enhances our students' overall literacy, providing essential "equipment for living," as Kenneth Burke put it. Both our core curriculum and this inaugural volume of *MCR* might be seen as responding to George Steiner's haunting question in his *My Unwritten Books* (2008): "What would be a core literacy adequate to the spiritual and practical needs of men and women on a multinational, increasingly intermeshed planet?" Undergraduate creative writing workshops (and publication venues such as *MCR*) exist, in part, to invite our students into conversations about the literate and the literary. We honor their presence in our classrooms and on these pages, inviting them (and all other comers) as full participants in literary and artistic communities.

In its varied contents, *MCR 2009* provides a template for future volumes, to which we invite submissions (for editorial information, see below). For example, visual art plays an integral role in this inaugural issue, which introduces the work of emerging artists Paige Freeseman (ceramic sculpture) and Sam Hitchcock (jewelry). In addition, Springfield's own Julie Blackmon, an internationally acclaimed photographer whose work has appeared in *The New Yorker*, *Oxford American*, and *National Geographic*, has graciously provided both cover art and a striking series of black-and-white photography on children and "the psychological domestic."

MCR 2009 is also unique in including a section entitled "Archival Treasures from the Ozarks." While literary annuals feature living authors as a matter of course, ours looks to "bring back" artists whose works lie languishing and largely forgotten. It is a simple if surprising fact that the Ozarks— presumably "hillbilly" hinterland cut off from citified "high" culture—has its share of manuscript and fine art collections, though in large part uncatalogued, under-studied, and unpublished. 2009, for example, marks the 100th birthday of the Kewpie, once termed "the greatest success . . . in the history of toys." That the Kewpie's creator, Rose O'Neill, lived and worked (and passed away) in the Ozarks remains fairly well known; that O'Neill was also a celebrated novelist, poet, and serious salon artist (holding fine-art exhibitions in New York and Paris) remains less well known. Virtually forgotten is O'Neill's social activism, particularly regarding woman's suffrage and woman's legal, social, sexual rights and identity. The David O'Neill Collection represents the nation's largest assemblage of her unpublished manuscripts, correspondence, and artwork; drawing from this local collection, we present an illustrated essay of O'Neill's "secret," sexualized, social-activist art.

For students of the craft of writing, two pieces will stand out. Shannon Wooden's interview with Kevin Brockmeier peers deeply into the latter's empathetic character-constructions (among other writerly topics). We also print a piece of private correspondence by Miller Williams (one-time Director of the University of Arkansas Press) to an aspiring poet, offering advice that remains useful for today's writers.

With this inaugural volume, the editors are pleased to offer two cash awards to contributors who are students or graduates of Missouri State University. **The *MCR 2009* Poetry Prize** is given to Satarah Wheeler for her poem, "The Sun, the Sea and the Small Things We Know." **The *MCR 2009* Prose Award** is given to Billy Clem for his personal essay, "Some Confirmation: A Gay Man Comes of Age in the Missouri Ozarks."

2. Some Information on Submissions.

MCR invites submissions for future issues; these will be considered during our open reading period each fall, typically from September to mid-November. All submissions are read, and members of the Missouri State University community (students, faculty, staff, and alums) are especially encouraged to send their best work. Authors and artists retain copyright over their work, though we'd appreciate acknowledgment of publication in *MCR*. At this time, electronic submissions are accepted for art only. Simultaneous submissions are fine as long as they are identified as such and notice is given if work is accepted elsewhere. A SASE is not needed; submissions are recycled and accept/regrets notice will be sent by email.

We accept submissions in most literary and visual-artistic genres: poetry, short story, creative nonfiction, personal essay, criticism, photography, free-form drawing, graphic design, illustration, and so on. Skillfully-rendered translation (of contemporary world literature particularly) is most welcome. Please note that "criticism" encompasses a wide range of subjects, styles, and approaches, from contemporary social/political commentary to literary-artistic analysis. The main criterion is readerly interest: criticism must be timely, accessible, free of jargon, and aimed at pleasing an "educated generalist" audience. (That is, critical work suited to *PMLA* or *CCC* is not suited to *MCR*.)

While not restricted to the following in subject matter, upcoming volumes will feature special themes:
MCR 2010 (ed. Lanette Cadle): Speculative Fictions
MCR 2011 (ed. Marcus Cafagña): Alumni Issue, highlighting
    work by faculty, students, and graduates of the College
    of Arts and Letters, Missouri State University
MCR 2012 (ed. Joel Chaston): Children's/Adolescent Art
    and Literature

For additional information about *MCR* and its imprint, *Moon City Press*, please visit our web page at http://english. missouristate.edu/moon_city_review.htm.

3. Acknowledgments.

We have many to thank. *MCR 2009* relies on underwriting by the Missouri State University College of Arts and Letters and Department of English; we thank Dean Carey Adams and our English Head, W.D. Blackmon, for their unwavering support. Michelle K. Nahon, an attorney-at-law and Missouri State University alum, has underwritten the two student/alum awards given in this present volume; we thank her for being "a friend of English."

Ben Pfeiffer, a graduate assistant in publications, helped compile and manage submissions, while Isaiah Vianese, Katherine Wertz, Jessica Glover, and Danielle Evans served as readers, making selections from a large gathering of work. Angelia Northrip-Rivera, Senior Instructor in English, performed her usual magic on the text layout, while Rebecca Sloane of University Printing Services helped in completing the cover design. Once more, Craig A. Meyer helped tighten the nuts and bolts. Lisa Wedekind of LightningSource made the tasks and technologies of printing seem deceptively easy. Tom Lavoie of the University of Arkansas Press continues to help professionalize our publications; given the resources U of Arkansas P puts at our disposal, Moon City could not ask for a better partnership.

The staff of Meyer Library's Special Collections and Archives—David Richards, Anne Baker, and Tracie Gieselman-Holthaus—have never failed us. They and Jimmie Allen, assistant professor of photography at Missouri State University, joined forces in reproducing most of the O'Neill images included here. David O'Neill gave us unfettered access to his collection of O'Neilliana, and Vernon D. Jordan, Jr. shared his considerable knowledge of Rose O'Neill's life, times, and art. For thus easing the scholar's burden, we give them all hearty thanks.

It is an honor to print the poetry of Michael Burns, professor emeritus of English, along with poems by his son and daughter. We take this opportunity to acknowledge his decades-long leadership of the creative writing program at Missouri State University: many of the students and alums—and faculty—published in this volume were at one time under his tutelage. We thank the entire creative writing faculty at Missouri State University for encouraging students to submit, giving special thanks to those faculty whose own work is represented here. And we thank the authors and artists who accepted our invitation to contribute, allowing all to experience "the kiss of print," as John Updike put it, alongside writers with differing levels of experience, but who all worked mightily to offer their best.

Accompanying his interview with Shannon Wooden, Kevin Brockmeier's essay, "I Remember 5 November 2008," first appeared in the British online journal, *Five Dials* 4 (Fall 2008): 7. We acknowledge the journal editor's courtesy in allowing us to reprint.

4. On the Naming of Moon City

So, where (or what) is the "Moon City" referenced in this old/new literary review? It's a question often posed, so we might oblige with a bit of Ozarks-style storytelling. (That the answer lies in the antics of railroad moguls only briefly disguises the underlying allegory, which pertains to a community's—and an academic small press's—"building of a name" for itself.) We begin with R. I. Holcombe's *History of Greene County, Missouri* (1883), a preeminent source on early Springfield—which, for a *very* brief time, was not one but two separate towns:[1]

> It may now be well to speak of the effect produced by the laying out of North Springfield—or "Moon City," as it was at first called. . . . Immediately before the old Atlantic and Pacific railroad (now the "Frisco") was completed to Springfield . . . a controversy arose in regard to the location of the depot. . . . A proposition was made by the company to run the road in on a survey that would bring the depot within a half mile

---

[1] For readability, the authors have occasionally modernized the punctuation and spelling of early texts.

of the Public Square, provided a certain sum should be raised. If this was not done, another route would be taken at least one mile north.

From here, let us detour through Jonathan Fairbank and Clyde Edwin Tuck's *Past and Present of Greene County, Missouri* (1915): "before the arrival of the road" in 1870, three local entrepreneurs (who had bought up the lands north of Springfield) "proceeded to make the following proposition to the railroad company: 'If . . . the depot be located upon our land, we will give the company a right-of-way two hundred feet wide; . . . also, we will lay out two hundred acres *into a town* and give the company an undivided half interest in it'" (emphasis added). Fairbank and Tuck continue:

> On the other hand, the railroad company was approached by delegations of merchants and property owners of Springfield, urging that the depot be located near the Public Square. . . . At length, early in December, 1868, two men reached Springfield as railroad commissioners, with authority to locate the depot and settle the question finally. These men were Andrew Pierce of Boston, Massachusetts, a typical New England Yankee, . . . and Thomas McKissick, a prominent railroad man of St. Louis. Several conferences were held by these gentlemen with the principal residents of the town . . . .
>
> "Your charter compels you to build into Springfield," said one prominent citizen to Andrew Pierce at the last of these meetings; "you *have* to build into Springfield, and we do not have to pay you one cent for doing it!"
>
> At that, Pierce leaped to his feet, and, smiting the table with his fist, shouted: "All right, that settles it. I'll very soon show you where I'll put that depot!"

"And he did," Fairbank and Tuck added, though—with typical gentility—they deleted the Yankee Pierce's cuss word (as reported elsewhere). By fiat, "'Moon City' (as the Old Town people were wont to call our town)" "sprang into existence *as if by magic*": so wrote George S. Escott in his *Directory of Springfield and North Springfield* (1878; emphasis added). If Escott is right—that it's the "Old Town people" who came up with the moniker—then it could not have been meant kindly.

It should be noted that, prior to 1870, several corporations had failed in their attempts to finance construction and conquer the difficult terrain. An article in the 27 June 1867 *Daily Missouri Democrat* (St. Louis) inventoried the assets of "Dinsmore and Company," which had contracted for part of the work; according to Arthur Paul Moser,[2] these assets amounted to "$266.67 in cash, four gold watches, a piano, and a set of spoons." Thus "the Southwest Company," the *Democrat* proceeded to declare, "had 'as much ability to build a railroad to the moon as to Springfield'" (Moser). When the railroad did arrive, this same derisive, pie-in-the-sky attitude transferred from the road to the town that would soon be built around it.

Returning to Holcombe's *History*, we read that "the new town developed a wonderful vitality, and was aided in all its enterprises by the railroad company," such that "a bitter rivalry arose between the two places":

> The company built an enormous frame hotel—the Ozark House—three stories in height, handsome in appearance and elegant in its appointments, which was destroyed by fire in the spring of 1875. As an offset to this, the citizens rallied to the assailed pride of "old town," and . . . erected the commodious,

[2] We quote from his unpublished typescript, "A Brief History of North Springfield Known as 'Moon City'" (1985), which resides in the Local History Department of The Library Center for Springfield-Greene County.

four-story brick structure known as the Metropolitan Hotel. In a thousand different ways, during the first few years succeeding the completion of the road, this antagonism [was] promoted. After it had been demonstrated that "old town" could not be "busted" and that "new town" could not be kept from growing, the hatchets were, by tacit agreement, buried.

As Holcombe declared, "the short, open space between the places has been gradually occupied," and "it will be but a brief period when it will require a sharp-sighted and well-informed person, indeed, to point out the line of demarcation between old Springfield and 'Moon City' or 'new town.'"

In 1887, just four years after Holcombe's writing, the separate townspeople voted to merge, making for a single Springfield. And Holcombe prophesied aright: if asked, few Springfieldians today could "point out the line of demarcation"—though aptly named Division Street—mainly because the story has been as good as forgotten.

And now for the moral of this story. Whether as a town or as a text, "Moon City" has always been an improvisation. It was, and it remains, a convenient fiction—an invention of entrepreneurs, a flight of fancy, a slap in the face of "old town" expectations, an upstart, Ozarks-style declaration. In its status as a literary-artistic annual (and as an academic small press of the same name), Moon City remains a mythic place, forever a "new town." Like the first railroad, it citifies an early pioneer settlement, bringing in fresh blood. Moon City remains a "place" (a press, a book annual) where Ozarks history and literary-artistic culture can be both remembered and reconstructed, engaging back-and-forth with the rest (and best) of the world "out there," bringing newcomers in, sending our own out and abroad, all interconnected—incorporated, as it were—through mutual interests in poetry, story, art, and criticism. The communities described in the beginning of this introduction find confirmation, if only symbolically so, in this conscious act of naming.

I. Featured Work

(Or: Some New Arrivals)

BURTON RAFFEL

Translation of Horace, *Odes 1.1*

Whoever knows
How long the gods want us to go on?
I don't, you don't, no one knows.
Don't look at astrological charts. Just wait. Things happen.
Another winter? No more winters? Who knows?
We see the sea breaking down the Tuscan coast:
Just watch, just wait, crush your grapes, and stop
Thinking, give up hoping, which never stops
But never arrives. Time has nothing to do with life;
It goes on going, even as we talk.

BURTON RAFFEL

God's Cherry Trees

If God grew cherry trees
in fields that He Himself
had planted, tilled, and watered
out of snow-white clouds,
His gorgeous fruit would hang
so heavy on those branches
leaves would drag the ground
and ripe perfume go drifting
down the air for miles
in all directions, no one
needing ladders for
the sweetest taste that any
tongue would ever know.
But who would come, and how,
though drawn by precious fragrance
men might surely die for?
Who would come, and how?

BURTON RAFFEL

Head-Lights

The worm that crawls majestically in circles,
quivering after ripened fruit, has come
around the world, unsatisfied, and landed
on my skull.
                    Demon lover,
wrapping leg by leg its length, lazy
in delight, antennae wriggling, insect
fur the green fluorescent light by which
we see it, indifferent, now, to every other
succulence, it slowly chews and bites.

BURTON RAFFEL

Elegance, Class

Whoever said elegance sat on its ass
smiling? Whoever boasted class
locked its knees and stamped
across the world?

Whoever saw grace as million grains of glass
in single movement, overpassing
peaceful moment, splashed
in crazy seas?

Whoever knew elegance as hoarded grace, stashed-up
woven bits of leap, of dash,
and all there is to class
that time, that dizzy silent moment?

Michael Czyzniejewski

The Pyromaniac Cast Away

Adrift, he is surrounded by water. Water in every direction, salty, blue, wet water. On this overcast day, the sun is hidden behind clouds—huge, vaporous pockets of water. The pyromaniac has given up hope. Three days after his plane plummeted to the sea, left alone and floating on his own seat, he decides he is doomed, that he'd rather fall to the depths than waste away. He will unclick his harness, use his remaining strength to roll over, and succumb.

Then he smells the embers. Somewhere, less than a mile away, burns a fire. Something has been lit, something wooden, and it calls out, siren-like. The pyromaniac contorts until he can see it, the rising black smoke, a dim haze in the air. Vigor for life renewed, he paddles across the waves, through choppy tide. He wants to see the fire, the actual flames, hear them and taste them, too. Even more, he wants to see what the fire is destroying, what it has already destroyed, be it a forest, a home, or something he only dares imagine—why would an island in the middle of the Pacific have a lumberyard? Yet he can see it. His arms move through the water faster than he has ever moved, his flotation device bobbing along, the fire growing closer with each stroke, but not nearly quickly enough.

As he approaches the shore, the pyromaniac witnesses a single palm tree aflame. It is split down the middle, and from the black streak lining the tear, the pyromaniac deduces lightning, a single bolt bifurcating the trunk, igniting the wood. The tree has not yet fallen, the two even pieces

6

somehow still upright, their large leaves burning, along with the bark and the flesh and the coconuts. The pyromaniac cannot believe his luck. It is as if fate is paying him back for what happened to his plane.

The pyromaniac treads the beach, closing on the flaming tree, until a fiery coconut flashes before him, inches from striking him in the head. The coconut bounces once in the sand, wobbles like a football, and comes to rest. Despite the pyromaniac's fear, the coconut's fire is not extinguished. He falls on all fours, placing his face a centimeter from the smoldering skin. The stench overwhelms him, a torched Thai restaurant, but the pyromaniac is transfixed: Black creeps down the surface, the brown hairs curling to orange, the singed skin bellowing into vapors. The pyromaniac can hear the liquid boiling inside. It excites him.

The pyromaniac stands and watches. Coconuts continue to plummet, the wood crackles, the flames inch downward. Three hours later, one of the halves topples, its twin just a few moments later, in the opposite direction. It is the most beautiful sight the pyromaniac has ever seen, a woman splayed across a bed, her legs scissored, only this is better. It is erotic, in a way no woman in a bed could ever be.

Once, while setting a house on fire, the pyromaniac found a baby inside a wooden crib. Several rooms already in flames, the pyromaniac entered the nursery and saw the crib, the driest of pine, its paint flaking, the cherry on his sundae. About to shake the last drops of gas from his can, the pyromaniac spied the baby's arms and legs and face, hair so black, skin so pink. The baby was alone and alive, abandoned the entire four hours the pyromaniac had scouted the house. Aside from a cough, smoke creeping through the vents, the baby seemed happy, relieved someone was finally there.

The pyromaniac dropped his can—his special can—and scooped up the child, an itchy blanket to cover its face, and glided down the stairs, out the front door and across the creaking, burning porch. On the lawn, the police awaited the trucks, sirens growing louder and louder, red lights flashing. The pyromaniac handed the baby to an officer, said he'd smelled the smoke, heard crying as he passed. He rushed in, never hesitating. It's what any decent person would do.

The parents, it turned out, had, that day, abandoned the child, leaving their baby to waste away in the wooden crib. They were arrested at the airport, pinned for endangerment and abandonment *and* the fire, while the pyromaniac was awarded an article in the paper, a snippet on the news, and a medal at a ceremony at a city council meeting. Had he not been a pyromaniac, had he not noticed the couple pack their car with suitcases to leave their dilapidated Cape Cod—no more than a glorified cardboard box—the baby would have died, suffering from starvation for days. That baby, now six years old and living with an aunt, writes the pyromaniac twice a year, sends photos, drawings, and letters. The pyromaniac burns them, watches them disintegrate, but not for the same reason he burns everything else.

The palm tree stops burning on the second day, and by that evening, the smoldering, even the smell, ceases. At this point, the pyromaniac realizes himself alone on the island, an island the size of a baseball diamond, its lone tree eliminated by the elements. The pyromaniac realizes he is dying. He is dehydrated, he is starving, and the island's only food source, coconuts, has burned. The pyromaniac counted thirty-six coconuts, making sure none escaped, tossing them all to the root of the tree, into the heart of the fire. Occasionally, a coconut would explode, discharging fruit and milk, and bits still lie in the sand, but not enough to sustain the pyromaniac, not for any length of time. All that remains of the island is sand, char, and the pyromaniac, engulfed by lots and lots of water.

The pyromaniac rescues his airplane seat from the surf and places it in the center of the island, next to the remains of the palm tree. He lies on his back, staring at the gray sky. Lightning flashes in the distance, thunder following each bolt. He can smell rain in the air. The pyromaniac begins to cry, hoping that someone, passing by, might hear.

Mind Games

(black and white work 2002-2004)

I have photographed my three children and their cousins and friends focusing on the subject of play. I am intrigued by play because the dark and mysterious sides to this make-believe world, as well as the heightened sense of beauty and awe, are fantastic elements that seem to parallel our own subconscious dreams, desires, and fears, no matter what age we are. The challenge for me is to photograph my children and others in an artistic alchemy allied to childhood imagination, and transform those familiar children to wonderful, fantastic beings that push the frontiers of the imaginations of the viewer—but, at the same time, ask that the viewer consider the wonder in everyday life.

Easy-Set Pool

Ice Cream Sandwich

11

Trampoline

Live Wire

12

Twirling

Dragon

Bubble Girl

Chalk

TED KOOSER

A Person of Limited Palette

I would love to have lived out my years
in a cottage a few blocks from the sea,
and to have spent my mornings painting
out in the cold wet rocks, to be known
as "a local artist," a pleasant old man
who "paints passably well, in a traditional
manner," though a person of limited
talent, of limited palette: earth tones
and predictable blues, snap-brim cloth cap
and cardigan, baggy old trousers
and comfortable shoes, but none of this
shall come to pass, for every day
the possibilities grow fewer, like swallows
in autumn. If you should come looking
for me, you'll find me here, in Nebraska,
thirty miles south of the broad Platte River,
right under the flyway of dreams.

MILLER WILLIAMS

Minds

And if there are minds
on Venus,
if the first of us finds
a rational genus
all penis,
and vulva, and squat,
and no word for love,
then what?

If there are such minds
past Mars,
if the first of us finds
movie stars
and oyster bars
again,
and no word for God,
what then?

Or we may call
as far
as we can fall,
by moon, by star,
what planets there are
and find
through limitless silence
no mind.

Then I think we could
in despair
think toward a god
(in hunger like prayer),
and love, and there
and then
invent them both
again.

BURTON RAFFEL

Comrade Stalin's Piano Concerto

The Henricka was housed in an ugly and very old building, ancient enough to have been blackened and seared by Napoleon when most of Moscow went up in flames. Over the years, as political tides regularly lapped and swirled, heaved and ebbed around all the structures of Russia, new and more appropriate lettering and decorations had been carved into the old building's portals and along its walls, inside and out; sooner or later, just as they had been put up, outmoded lettering and decorations had been chiselled away. Late in the nineteenth century—by then the building had become a landmark, though it could never have been anything but nondescript—the Henricka had been taken over by the Metropolitan, leader of the Russian Orthodox Church, and had remained consecrated to such spiritual uses as interested first one Metropolitan and then another, until the Orthodox Church was abruptly dispossessed by the Revolution. Because such things were too expensive to remove, there were still empty niches in the Henricka's walls, where icons had once stood; perhaps because no one had ever quite noticed them, or stopped to wonder to what use they might better have been put, here and there all up and down the dim corridors there were still heavy marble pedestals, no longer supporting great basins for holy water or founts for baptism. Hats and occasionally umbrellas were now all they ever held. After 1918, the Henricka's broad, squat, rather lumpy shape, with its dirty rectangular stones and worn marble floors, had stood empty for a time: the

Revolution had first to endure war and starvation, had first to fight off counter-revolution, and finally establish itself as a permanently flaming Red island in a sea of perpetual Capitalist sharks. And then, in the early 1920s, the Henricka had finally become what it remained thereafter, a cultural center; early Bolsheviks thought the transformation particularly fitting, since as they viewed things, culture was to the Mind (and also to the Revolution) as, once, religion had been to the Masses.

But the Henricka had not come into its true glory, or even taken on its current name, until after the Great War Against Hitler. Fresh plaster and new paint had of course helped in this post-war renewal. Still, the central fact of the Henricka's new glorification had not been any merely physical improvement, but Yuri Tamashev's appointment as Director. Tamashev had been a music student, before the war, an adequate pianist, a decent violist, not much of a composer, but a superb organizer. His talents, though he had not then realized it, were far more useful for presenting than for producing art. They were very real, not to say splendid, talents, aided and abetted by a dry sense of humor, a good way with words and women, and an abiding admiration for good art that was quite as strong as his abiding distaste for the bad variety. By one of those minor miracles that, even in totalitarian societies, work small but very real miracles, he turned out to be the ideal square peg in the carved square hole.

Only his distaste for bad art might, in the event, have been expected to get him into trouble, for, like him, it had managed to survive the war more or less intact. But in truth the war cured all such difficulties in advance: the left arm that once-Lieutenant Tamashev had lost to the Hitlerian hordes virtually guaranteed him the kind of absolute protection few Soviet citizens, and no prior Director, ever possessed. Its state-sanctified and intensely visible non-presence (for

Tamashev finally rejected every prosthetic device known to Soviet science, wearing his loss, as it were, on his pinned-back sleeve) glittered more brightly than any cluster of medals, and could be plainly identified from even further away. And Tamashev's own wryly, wearily intelligent nature helped him make full use of that status. Henricka, indeed, had been the name of his first mistress, after the war, and he was glad to be able to remember her as, in those years of rediscovering Life and Art, she had been. Henricka in the flesh was a mediocre musician, a soprano whose vibrato tended to wobble and whose pitch was more variable than even a loyal lover liked, and for that as well as other reasons the Siberian provinces had soon claimed her. But her musically uncertain flesh had unquestionably been passionate and, before acquiring its ownership and use, Tamashev had suffered sufficiently, through a series of operations and clumsy rehabilitative procedures, so that her sheer physical opulence had more or less permanently touched him. He who could no longer play any instrument (it had been suggested that he take up the trumpet, which could be held by one hand, but he refused to take the suggestion seriously) was moved to discover that the instrument which was his own body, at least, remained capable of quite astonishing and distinctly artistic effects. He was forever grateful to the lady. Even knowing that her actual tombstone stood in Omsk—or was it Novosobirsk? he was no longer sure—did not detract from his faintly sentimental sense of the architectural Henricka as a fitting memorial to those days of rediscovered pleasure, those nights of inventive bliss. He certainly knew that it did no harm to let oneself be guided, from time to time, by faintly sentimental visions. Who could set reliable boundaries between Art and Sentiment—and what was the one, in any case, without the other?

The Henricka itself could not have been so readily characterized, in Western terms. It was, among other things, a concert hall, a recital auditorium, and a political club; for those with the proper elevated status it was also a restaurant, something very like a hotel, and of course a brothel. It housed a branch of the Writer's Union, which published a newsletter that was, in fact, a well-read literary magazine. From time to time it was home to art exhibitions; folk dance troupes and even a stray ballet company or two had thumped and pirouetted on its rather narrow and excessively flexible stage (the ancient wooden beams were sagging and long since in need of replacement, though it was understood they would have to collapse before they could be replaced). The ageless babushkas who swept the Henricka's floors and, sometimes, cleaned its windows, never knew (or cared) what denizens of the world of Art might pass through the damp corridors. Comrade Tamashev was their Leader, and where he led they followed, not so much blindly as mindlessly. One functioning mind per organization was quite enough; more than that, and trouble could and somehow invariably did set in. Even the Revolution had not changed that.

Marfa Grigorevna, of course, saw things differently. She was a pianist, for one thing: no one could have mistaken her rather slight figure for a solid, column-like babushka shape. More important, although she was bright-eyed and pretty, she spoke very little, she laughed not at all, and though she was the Henricka's current house pianist she did not, like those who had come before her, attend other functions as well. She had not once been seen on a Party functionary's arm; she had not once been seen sipping a glass of vodka; and, most astonishing, it was pretty clearly understood that—though married to somebody or other, and so quite accustomed to having a man in her bed—she had not once shared any such accommodation with Director Tamashev. It was universally and accurately understood, since babushkas have their own sources of knowledge, that Director Tamashev had more than once indicated the propriety, even the necessity, of such extra-professional activities, but had been consistently rebuffed. Babushkas know such things, but cannot understand them. They did not pretend to understand Marfa Grigorevna, though they were confident that people like her, and most especially women like her, did not, like Director Tamashev or the Henricka, last forever.

Her worst rebuff of their Director, however, would if they had known it been quite beyond either their knowledge or comprehension. But it had been, until she was forced to countermand it, entirely between Tamashev and herself.

"And now, now, it's time for Comrade Stalin to hear you," he had announced to Marfa Grigorevna, early in her pianistic tenure. It was Tamashev, inevitably, who had chosen her for that post—which indeed had not existed until he created it, just before offering it to her. Though at twenty-two or three she already had a large reputation for difficulty and unreliability (that is, politically: musically she rarely missed a note), one exposure to her music-making had persuaded him that, with proper management, this young woman could be a star not only on the large stage of the Soviet Union but on the still larger one of the glorious, largely unknown world outside. There were immensely positive gains to be had, playing on that stage, both for the actual performer and also for those who arranged performances. Yuri Tamashev had not hungered and thirsted for those material pleasures; his country had lived so long in its isolation that he was not even precisely sure what they were. But neither was he the man to ignore them, once they swam, entirely of their own accord, into his ken. Naturally, in spite of her undeniable gifts Marfa Grigorevna had never been offered the chance to play on any such farflung stage; only someone as politically secure as Tamashev could have opened the possibility for her, and most men thus protected did not trouble themselves with trivialities like music. What Tamashev had initially offered, when he took her on at the Henricka, was in her terms quite valuable enough: a steady income and an opportunity not only to perform regularly but to perform pretty much the repertoire that, at any given moment, particularly interested her. She could go where she wanted, musically speaking, he explained, and she knew he was speaking truthfully: that was quite a striking enough offer, in the choking, Byzantine cobwebs of the Soviet Union, to promptly secure her services. And then, when she had been performing at the Henricka for three months—alone, in chamber groups, as accompanist to a number of singers, and several times with a small orchestra—Tamashev unexpectedly conjured up what he called, matter of factly, the Stalin option.

Her response to this proposal too had been immediate. "No!"

She did not smile; her revulsion was quite unconcealed.

"He's too old to eat you," he had said with a small chuckle, well aware, despite her rejection of his own proposals, that she had not been prompted by mere sexual horror.

She did not reply.

In the half dozen years of his reign, Tamashev had had occasional, but strictly limited exposure to Comrade Stalin. The Henricka flourished, but not quite on the Dictator's scale. Stalin had come to performances, now and then; he had been approving; more important, he had never levelled a single disapproving (and thus of course fatal) word or gesture against performance, performer, or empressario. For all his secure status, Tamashev knew better than to unnecessarily push himself or any of his charges. He had been and he remained an artist at heart; that heart was not unduly ambitious, and the art-serving pleasure he took in doing what he did was one of his more notable virtues. But Marfa Grigorevna's way with Mozart was like nothing he had ever heard, and he knew what Comrade Stalin liked. The Dictator might enjoy, as he notoriously did, poor musical taste, and be possessed of virtually no musical knowledge.

It was universally understood that what Stalin liked to hear were vigorous, linear melodies supported by straightforward, bland harmonies: a Soviet Johann Strauss, had there been one, would have found himself fairly draped in medals and other, larger-sized rewards. The Dictator also liked women in lowcut dresses; predictably, he was known to be fond of evenings lush with can-can dancing, sparkling with music of suitably similar shimmer and shine. But for some reason he also adored Mozart, and in particular Mozart's piano concertos, and he had made it his business to hear them often enough, and listen to them closely enough, so that his poor taste had become, in this one nook and cranny of music, irrelevant. When it came to Mozart piano concertos, Comrade Stalin *knew* what was good, and *liked* what was good, and there was not a doubt in Tamashev's mind that, given the opportunity, his approval would include Marfa Grigorevna's performances. Early Mozart, middle Mozart, late Mozart: it did not matter, she displayed every aspect of the master's genius with power and brilliance, yet without the slightest strain. She was, in a word, magnificent, and the Dictator would be, in a word, ecstatic. And that would of course do no harm to anyone.

But Tamashev had thoroughly researched Marfa Grigorevna's history: it was the least he could do, to protect both himself and all those who served and were served by the Henricka. He knew far more about her than his pianist dreamed, and he knew that, in this matter above all others, she could be expected to be difficult. The obvious arguments for soothing the Kremlin's Wild Beast would have persuaded at least ninety-nine of a hundred musicians, but he knew they probably could not persuade her. But once she had recoiled from the idea, and perhaps to keep himself from having to do what he truly did not want to have to do, Tamashev proceeded to trot out for Marfa Grigorevna the standard arguments. A child could have marshalled them just as well; they were familiar to virtually everyone. He was not a crass man: if, given a few moments to realize what she would really be doing by refusing to cooperate, she would yield decorously, he preferred to give her—and himself— that opportunity. The dirty-handled lever he held in reserve was not one he would enjoy using. So he said, first,

"_____

_____

_____." "

"No," she replied just as emphatically.

Nodding quietly, he proceeded to the next of the standard arguments, saying, bluntly (because he still hoped that bluntness might somehow accomplish what the words themselves probably could not),

"_____

_____." "

"No," she said again. "No!" He could see she was angry, now, rather than horrified. Had there been anyone else present, she might well have sealed her fate: Tamashev knew that the great poet, Osip Emielevitch Mandelstam, had been irrevocably condemned because of a scribbled poem insulting the Dictator, and others had died and were still dying for even less. If she had turned to leave, he would have had to restrain her. He sighed, and nodded, and moved to the third and perhaps weightiest conventional argument of all, explaining tersely that

"_____." "

This was weighty indeed, and Tamashev could see how pale she grew.

"No," she said at last, facing him militantly. "Not even then. He is a butcher, he is a coward, and I will not play for him. Never!"

Tamashev nodded sadly. Of course, Comrade Stalin was a butcher, and he might very well have been a coward as well, but what did that have to do with performing Mozart, who himself had not been a particularly savory character? If Salieri had not poisoned his musical rival and superior, perhaps he should have, as in Pushkin's poem, "Mozart and Salieri," he was shown doing. And what were even Mozart and Salieri— what was music itself—in the face of all the perfectly clear opportunities that playing for the Dictator were likely to produce, precipitating foreign tours and foreign fame and who could say what else out of the Soviet sky, pouring down on both of them like Danaean showers of gold?

So calmly, though with genuine regret, he turned to the one argument that, knowing Marfa Grigorevna, he had small doubt would work. The information had been obtained just that week. He had hoped, hoped most profoundly, not to have to use it. But he had not deceived himself: an iron will could only be bent by a crow bar.

"But just think," he said slowly, giving her time to appreciate exactly what he was saying, "how much Comrade Stalin, if he approved of your performance, as I'm sure he will, would be able to do for your son."

What he now saw on her face was more than pallor: Tamashev knew his unspoken message had been entirely clear. She had not suspected he knew anything of her personal, non-Henricka existence, but there had indeed been a son in her inconspicuous marriage. And if she did not agree to gratify Comrade Stalin's harmless affection for Mozart, then Tamashev could, or he would, as a loyal citizen of the Soviet state ... oh, she knew what he could and what, given her own and her family's experience, she was sure he would do—for why else would he have mentioned the child, why else would he have so carefully saved this information as the trump card he plainly knew it to be? If she had been wrong about Tamashev, if until this very moment she had trusted him far more than he deserved, she now knew better. But it was now too late.

"I would suggest," he said gently, feeling something of the horror she had forced him to conjure up, "perhaps the twentieth concerto, in C Minor—though, of course, it is for you and you alone to decide, Marfa Grigorevna. You cannot make a wrong decision, in these matters. I rely on you, you have my absolute confidence."

She had not spoken; she had not needed to. It was settled. When he mentioned a possible date, she simply nodded. Of course: in any event, Comrade Stalin would himself be the final authority. Whatever date, whatever time, whatever day: the Dictator and he alone would decide. But Marfa Grigorevna would play. And, being the kind of musician she was, she would play well, she could not help herself. She would play Mozart, and later on, he suspected, she would play other things as well. He was sorry, but he was also relieved: a man who had been permitted to live as long as he had, a man who had managed to arrive at his station in life, only because German guns had blown off one of his arms, could not be excessively sentimental or delicate. Given what was at stake, he could not be expected to decline the use of appropriate, strategic, effective force. Had she been in his position, would Marfa Grigorevna have simply shrugged and surrendered? He did not think so.

Her husband seemed to have been born a philologist; his life was spent happily tracking obscure Khirgizian roots to their even more obscure proto-historical origins. He loved his work, as he loved her and their child, but his frontiers extended no further. His parents had been peasants, and illiterate, which was why, even in the very worst of times, he had never experienced political trouble of any kind. Indeed, unlike most Soviet citizens, he could have gone on to advanced studies in anything he liked: he was intelligent, he was disciplined, but most important of all, for any career in the Soviet Union, his background was absolutely impeccable, seamlessly proleterian as far back as the memory of man could recall. He could have risen in the Party; he could easily have become a ruler, rather than remaining one of the ruled. But neither ruling nor being ruled had ever concerned him. Perhaps that was why Marfa Grigorevna had married him: as Tamashev's research had informed him, both her parents, two of her older siblings, and more relatives and friends than anyone wanted to count had died, one way or another, at the Dictator's hands. From the earliest moment of consciousness, even before she had propelled herself to the piano keyboard and clung there, as to a life raft, the world had seemed to her a pressingly threatening gibbet, worked by a puppet master who relished his task, squeezing life out of the little figures he plucked from an apparently endless, maliciously cultivated heap. Her music was just as divorced from the main currents of their time as her husband's lists of verbs and declensions, but her life remained irrevocably tethered to affairs of state, twisted into a hard, perpetually bleeding knot. The gibbet's shadow was always there, even when the glare of high noon would have made other shadows invisible. It was a shadow cut so deeply into her existence that its dark visibility no longer depended on exterior illumination.

"Just play," he advised her. She had never heard him raise his voice; he was in his way a passionate man, but the quasi-divine star he had been born and raised under seemed to have left him immune to all the forms of anger that ran, often like wildfire, from her hair to the very tips of her fingers. "Mozart, Beethoven, anything. A concert is a concert. Don't look up. You don't have to know who's listening to you. What difference does it make?"

There was a huge linguistic atlas open in front of him. He was leaning toward it, the better to make out maps and charts, because they were sharing the single reading lamp. She sat on the other side of the small table, curled into a wooden chair, not worrying whether she could see what she was doing, her head bent, darning little shirts and stockings, jabbing with her needle as if she were an executioner rather than a repairman.

"Yes, and if he sends for me, afterward?" She tried to keep her voice calm, tried to keep from making a scene. "What if I have to go to the royal box and let him admire me?"

He shook his head quietly.

"No matter what, Marfa, Stalin's only a man, and by now an old man at that. And a busy man. You won't have to make conversation with him. Thirty seconds, at most, and it will all be over. You'll see."

She caught herself just before the needle angrily impaled her thumb.

"And if he speaks to me?"

He shrugged.

"If you have to, you answer. A 'yes' or a 'no', dropped into the well of history, won't mean anything, won't hurt anybody. Would your father want you to spit in his face? Would your mother tell you to insult him? What good would that do?"

She sat, needle poised, wishing it were a sword and she could crucify the Dictator on it, shove it straight through his blood-gorged heart.

"You don't know," she murmured. "How could you know?"

He turned a page, slowly, and she thought he would not reply. Indeed, what could she expect him to say?

"I don't, no," he said at last. Through the concrete walls, that should have been solid and soundproof but were somehow as porous as paper, she could hear, on all sides, the noises of other families, other mothers, other fathers, other children. They were all packed into their apartments like mice in a multi-storied cage. Laboratory mice, for the Great Man's experiments. "Would you want me to? Do you want Ilya to know? Do you want to be hung over his life, like an eternal pall, the way your parents, the way your whole family, have always hung over yours? Yes?"

She surprised even herself by the steady calm with which she answered him:

"'Life is irrational', you always say. 'Words are irrational. Music is irrational'. Why should I pretend I'm not irrational too?"

He smiled his most beatific smile, and she wondered if, after all, *that* wasn't what she had married him for, the sight of that steady, reassuring beacon, piercing and brightening any stormy sea? He did not have to agree with her, to make her supremely grateful. He just had to be there: in her world, that was more than enough.

"Why pretend anything?" he said with that academic placidity he could not help assuming whenever serious subjects were discussed. Ideas were not consequences, for him. Raised out of the barnyard as he had been, he still saw discussion as a harmless game, debate as a healthy exercise. "Just play, Marfa. You know, when I was first in school I hated it. 'Why do I have to stay inside there?' I used to ask, because I wanted to go outside and play, the way I used to. And my mother, who didn't know one letter from another, thank God she always said the same thing: 'Just stay. You'll find out why'. And I did. She didn't have to be an educated woman to know more than I did. If she'd let me run away, she would have made a great mistake. But she didn't. And now I'm glad she didn't."

She nodded slowly.

"You know I'll play."

He bent closer to his book.

"I know. So do you. But first you have to fight yourself like this. You think I don't know? After five years of being married to you? For shame. Of course I know. But when you

30

fight with you, I can't even be a referee. I can only watch: that's all."

Head down, facing but not seeing the objects she was darning, she almost smiled—not quite, but almost. After a moment her needle began to ply once more. If her hands were equally willing when she came out on stage and sat at the piano, if her eyes did not drown themselves in tears, the whole thing was truly settled, now: she would play for Him. She said nothing. What good were words? She had said what she could say. Now she had to do what she could do. She hoped she could do what she knew she had to—for her own sake, for her husband's, but especially for her son's. They both trusted her, the child implicitly, the husband on the basis of reason, thought, experience. On the basis of love. Was he right? She hoped he was—or, at least, she *thought* she hoped so. But she did not know even that for sure. No medieval Christian, commanded to perform for the Devil in Hell's brightly lit auditorium, could have suffered more pain or felt more turmoil. God Himself could declare the performance necessary, even good, and she could not believe it, she would never have taken the declaration at its Word. But she would play. She would play. Somehow.

She did not worry about rehearsals: music was not (and never had been) the source of her difficulties. Even knowing the occasion for which she had to prepare, she did what had to be done and went about it in exactly the same way she always did. It helped, too, that she had wrapped an aura of unreality about the whole thing, an inchoate but powerfully pulsing sense that, at the last moment, it simply would not happen—something, or someone, would surely stop it. This same sense had frequently protected her, as a child facing certain punishments or unavoidable ordeals. Only when the pretense could be entertained no longer, when the switch was descending or the examiner was actually entering the room, was she obliged to let reality take place—a sudden, unexplainable, utterly unaccountable burst of worldly hostility that, breaking thus unexpectedly over her head, could not, of course, have been either foreseen or forestalled. "Better to die of a heart attack than slowly, by inches," she remembered hearing her ailing grandfather whisper, while engaged in dying as slowly and painfully as inadequate medical practice and an implacably hostile State could possibly have provided. She had vowed never to let herself die by slow degrees, or with her eyes open. "It's better not to know," she had always told herself, and she did her best to keep knowledge away. "What you don't know can't hurt you," was the operating motto, especially since, without fail, what she did know *did* hurt her. It always had; she was confident it always would. Nor had her confidence ever been misplaced.

Yuri Tamashev did not attend her rehearsals, as on earlier occasions he sometimes had. He was affable, even cordial, when they met; he did not press her on any subject whatever. Nor did he ask her questions, or consult her on details. In a word, he too acted as if the scheduled concert would somehow be unscheduled, by Heavenly fiat, before it had to actually take place. The Henricka never did much by way of advance notice to its patrons; this time it did nothing at all. Publicity was never needed, for Soviet cultural events; for events attended by Comrade Stalin it was neither needed nor wanted. There were no posters to worry her, no external signs that anything at all was to happen.

And, in the interim, she did what all Soviet citizens learn to do: she survived.

"You're not nervous," she said to herself, listening to the Haydn symphony that was the first piece on the program. And it was true: nervous upset was not what was troubling her. It was almost true that nothing was troubling her—or at least nothing she was aware of, nothing she would let herself be aware of. The murderer of eight million *kulacks*, the Great Leader who had led his country into a war in which twenty-four million of its citizens had died, the Dictator who had been responsible for her parents' deaths, for her older brother's, for her older sister's, responsible as well for the death of two uncles on her mother's side, and another on her father's, the feared and fearful Patriarch who had, as her husband put it, hung over her crib like a Devil's icon—Stalin, Lord and Ruler of all he surveyed—was sitting in one of the two small box seats, toward the rear of the Henricka's modest-sized auditorium. He was watching Mikhail Pompanock, born in Kiev, trained in Leningrad, conduct the small orchestra. Mostly, of necessity, he was watching Pompanock, for the orchestra was almost entirely out of sight, their more usual role being that of a large pit band for activities visible on the stage behind and above them. That stage was not suitable for an orchestra, Pompanock maintained. It was large enough, but placing instrumentalists so high, relative to the acoustic back line, ruined the sound. "There's no counterpoint from up there," he had insisted, "and if you kill counterpoint, you've killed the goose that lays your golden eggs." Director Tamashev had not argued. It was indeed his policy, exactly as he had told her, to let his artists choose their own venues. The artists left scheduling, or the making of travel arrangements, or appeals to the bureaucracy (for a new harp, for repairs to seats, for the purchase of scores), to him. He left the music-making to them.

It was good music-making. The country seemed to be full of brilliant instrumentalists. The first-chair players in this more or less pickup orchestra were all soloists, some with long recording histories, and the second- and even third-chair players were virtually as good. String section tonal unity is said to take years of hard work; this group had achieved it, apparently effortlessly, at the first rehearsal. The first-trumpet would have been a headliner in any hall in the world; the principal clarinetist, who would never be heard on a recording or in any but a Soviet setting (his father having been executed during the war, and his mother having died in a prison camp, and he therefore permanently politically suspect), had achieved at age thirty a smooth legato sweep that most clarinetists could only dream about. And for all their superb competence, they paid attention to Pompanock, they were intensely respectful of Papa Haydn, and had she really been able to listen to it, the symphony would have been a joy and a delight. No true musician could tire of such music, nor had she. But she could not really hear anything but the fact of it, the sheer, palpable presence of Haydn, who on this night would come before Mozart as he came before him into the world. And then it would be her turn.

And then it was her turn. She was ushered onto the stage, in traditional style, by Mikhail Pompanock. She bowed automatically, a quick dipping of her head: there were after all hundreds of people out there, not just Him. She dropped onto the piano bench, making no last-minute adjustments. She was barely aware of sitting alone on the stage, of being positioned more prominently than even the traditional soloist: the audience could see her at the keyboard, and they could see Pompanock's back and his moving arms, and that was essentially all they could see.

Pompanock looked at her, she nodded, he lifted his arms, it began, the long surging chords of the introduction. She had not consciously realized that the piano was to enter when, astonished, she realized that the piano already *had* entered, that she was playing, leaning into the sparkling transition passages, rippling energetically through her opening arpeggios, focussing down into the delicate fingering of the first melody, high and bright and clear in the right hand. The whole first movement was a dazzle of incoherent sensation, but she trusted her fingers, and they carried her through. The slow movement, with its accelerating, rapid central portion, and then the dashing rondo of the final movement—it was all a timeless, inevitable working out, cast in rhythmic steel two hundred years earlier, needing only to be unrolled, spread out, exhibited. There was no more consciousness in her playing than there was in her, as she sat there on the stage, exposed to His eyes, flattering His ears. But though it was not conscious, it was excruciating, it was pure pain: if she had been obliged to stay aware of every malevolent atom, she would have fainted, she might have died. She survived; she sat, she played, she finished—damp with exertions she did not remember making, weak with sensations she could barely fight off, pale with she did not know what anxiety. What was still to come? That was the most brutal question of all.

She found her way off the stage, back on the stage, off the stage, back on the stage. Whatever Pompanock wanted her to do, she did. Whatever anyone had wanted her to do, she would have done. And then, somehow, she was walking beside Pompanock, and Yuri Tamshev was on her other side, and they moved through the parting sea of the audience, like Pharoh's chariots nearing the Red Sea, they approached the box, and then she was standing in front of him, and he was saying something, and the roaring in her ears was not the audience—which had become totally silent—and she could not understand anything but the low, somewhat halting sound of His voice. Words.

"Thank you, Comrade Stalin," she heard Tamashev saying. He said something else, she did not know what. And then His voice spoke once more, and this time, as if by some magical transformation, she heard the words, she understood:

"There is a recording of this, I assume?"

"Of course," she heard Tamashev answer, after the faintest of hesitations.

"I would appreciate a copy," He went on.

Tamashev promised to deliver on the next day. And then, somehow, He had turned, He was leaving, He was gone. They led her away, back stage, to the small antechamber used as a dressing room. She fell into a chair. Pompanock was scowling, Tamashev seemed nervous.

"Tell the orchestra," Tamashev said. "Extra pay, of course."

Pompanock grimaced.

"Idiot!"

"What else could I say?" Tamashev was not in fact apologetic; he knew he was right. "There she is, fainting with horror. She won't speak to him. What else could I have done?"

"It's impossible," Pompanock said. "Look at her."

"She will do it," Tamashev said quietly. "And so will the rest of you. So will I. Excuse me, I need to alert the manufacturing plant, they will have to call in a crew.' He made a wry face. "Half my budget for the rest of the year," he said simply. "But could I say no to Him?" He looked at the conductor. "Could *you*?"

Pompanock looked at his watch.

"We will play the second half of the concert. We will take a ten-minute rest. Then we will start to record. I leave the rest to you."

He left. After a minute, so too did Tamashev, perhaps to make his telephone call. She understood without understanding. She would now have to play the concerto again, and again, and always for Him. It would all be for Him, she and all the others, impelled only by fear of what He could and perhaps would do, by knowledge of what He had already done.

And she shuddered, feeling as if she had been possessed, taken over, by some lurking incubus. It had not asked her leave, it had simply occupied her. And it would never leave her. She was His, now: he owned her as surely as if he had

36

wound a chain around her wrist and tied it to his belt. Marfa Grigorevna was now Comrade Stalin's musical toy. He would wind her up, He would tell her when and what to play, and she would have to play, for there were no choices, there were no alternatives. In His world there was only His will, and death. She would have chosen the grave, had she been able to. She could not; even if only because of her son, she could not, but it was more than Ilya, it was more than her husband, it was more than everything she cherished and remembered and longed for. She would do His will, now and forever.

There was a movement in her throat, like something struggling to get to her lips, to rip its way out. Was that strange, strangled sound meant to be a scream? Her hands found their way to her high-piled hair, pulled. Her hair tumbled down, the long steel pin was clutched in her fingers, and then, as if guided by some robotic machine, it tore open first one wrist and then the other. Blood pulsed out, her head swam. She dropped the pin, she closed her eyes. What she herself could not do, her hands had done for her, as earlier in the evening her hands had played for her. They had done what had to be done. Her eyes stayed closed, her head drooped to the side, her hands hung loose, the blood flowing more slowly, now, for there was not much left to pour out.

When Yuri Tamashev returned, a quarter of an hour later, her body was already growing cold. He had seen many dead bodies, he knew. But what could he do? What could he have done?

John Dufresne

The Wood Inside

When the earth finally thawed last spring, it was opening week of rainbow season on the Big Wilson, and we buried the Easter animals that Dad had wrapped in tin foil and stacked in his freezer alongside Hector Papineau's dressed-out venison: the pair of Muscovy ducklings from the Ben Franklin's in Guilford who caught pneumonia, Mom said, from sleeping out on the back porch; Simone's cozy Leghorn chick, Lulu, whose eyes leaked green syrup, and whose beak softened to oatmeal; and my Belgian hare, Jake, who'd gnawed nearly through the clawfoot leg on Mom's wardrobe before choking on a splinter, digging at his neck, tearing through his fur, skin, and sinew, trying to reach the wood inside.

Mom's husband George dropped us by Dad's on his way fishing. Simone and I ate Sugar Pops and watched TV at the kitchen table while Dad showered and dressed. We watched cartoons. Simone kept her mittens on. In his bedroom, Dad answered a phone call and spoke quietly to whoever it was. I carried our milky bowls to the sink and set them in an inch of sudsy, gray water beside the two glasses. I took a Marlboro from the box on the counter, slipped it in my shirt pocket. Took the book of matches, too. From the Dog Sled Tavern. We watched that coyote blow himself to smithereens again with a tube of Acme dynamite.

We buried our animals off the path in the woods that leads down to the Bowditch farm. Buried them wrapped like candies three feet deep by the speckled alders. Dad tamped the dirt with the rusted blade of his spading fork. I said a prayer to St. Francis. Simone hugged Dad's leg and sniffled. He smoothed her hair. She closed her eyes. We drove to the Dixfield Diner. Dad does all his talking in public.

We sat in a booth. Silver and blue vinyl seats. The diner smelled like Dutch Cleanser. Simone and I sat across from Dad. He wore the plaid, flannel shirt we'd bought for him last Christmas. Dad joked about mud season with Mary Moody, our waitress. I could see Dad's reflection in the window, see the back of his head like the dark side of the moon. And beyond his reflection, I could see George's pickup parked across the street outside Ledoux's Olde Tyme Inn. Dad told Mary he'd have two eggs sunnyside, bacon, and wheat toast. And give the kids whatever they want. Two chocolate milks and two grilled cheese sandwiches.

Simone kicked her feet against our booth, blew chocolate bubbles through her straw. Dad hung his spoon from his nose to make Simone laugh. He saw me staring at his hand and at the space where a finger used to be. He smiled, touched the back of my hand with his fingertips, drew a circle. Dad sponged the yoke with his toast, ate the toast, clapped the crumbs from his hands. He sipped his coffee and watched Mary Mooney slide a dish of apple pie from the glass dispenser at the counter. He sat up straight. And then he started talking.

After my father left, quit Sawyer's Home Heating Oil, and moved to Delaware, that's when Donny Morin told me we could have saved the Easter animals, could have stuffed them with sawdust like his old man did with the twenty-three inch rainbow he's got mounted over the sofa in their trailer. Donny watched him do it. You scrape what's inside, all that damp and shiny stuff, and then whatever it is will last forever. That's the way it works. Donny said his old man said you only get to keep what's gone.

Ursula

FADE IN:

Devils Lake, North Dakota. The Thirties. Series of shots. The young principal of the elementary school steps out with URSULA USREY. Ursula's parents Nelson and May had died of exposure a few years earlier when they lost their way home from church in a blizzard. Ursula is very much in love with MR. HEERMAN, but he doesn't necessarily wish to marry, to settle down. He's married, he likes to say, to his job. He needs to devote all his energies to the children and to the town. He also dates FRIEDA TOFTHAGEN, but only on occasion, and only casually.

With Ursula, he talks about philosophy and education (Whitehead and Dewey), about the dangers of that socialist Roosevelt and about the social ills at the Indian agency. He reads the Bible aloud to her. She reads Emily Dickinson to him. In a few years, he tells her, he'll enter politics. Maybe one day run for governor. He says it out loud: Governor Arthur Clement Heerman. He lifts his brow. Ursula smiles, tries to picture herself in Bismarck. When Frieda gets pregnant, Mr. Heerman marries her. He buys a large Victorian on 2nd Street with the financial help of her uncle Emery Mapes, the man who invented Cream of Wheat, a house not far from school. He settles into domesticity.

Ursula, of course, is heartbroken. She knows that everyone in Devils Lake pities her, and she can't abide that. But she is still in love. Mr. Heerman hires her at the school— she is, after all the brightest woman he knows. Eventually,

Ursula becomes accustomed to this new arrangement, this different kind of intimacy. She is very much Mr. Heerman's wife at school. She is in charge. The other teachers, a young man from St. Paul, who is effeminate and is stern with his pupils, and a young woman, a girl really, who is a great favorite of her students, defer to Ursula.

Mr. Heerman and Frieda raise three boys. When the boys are ready for college, Frieda dies in childbirth. Ursula arrives to comfort Mr. Heerman and his sons. She arranges care for the baby, manages the funeral, ensconces herself daily in the Victorian home as the choreographer of grief and condolences. Over the ensuing weeks, she cooks meals, sees to the children's well-being, supervises the nanny. She stays late to sit up and read to the bereaved widower, and soon they have fallen into their old conversations about the meaning of life. Ursula believes that once a seemly length of time has passed, Mr. Heerman will see that he needs a wife, a caretaker, a helpmeet and boon companion.

She begins to plan for the inevitable and desirable upheaval in her life. She sells off some furniture. She speaks with Mr. James Lamb, Realtor, at the Odd Fellows Lodge about the possible sale of her home. Mr. Heerman returns to work and asks the young teacher, no longer a girl, now in her mid-thirties, to marry him. Ursula is devastated. She walks out into a wheat field. She wonders how her life could have possibly come to this. She imagines her future—empty and endless. Barren, infertile, lonely. She becomes the subject of cautionary tales that mothers tell their daughters. Pitiable. Would that she could leave, begin all over somewhere else.

The young wife drowns herself in Sweetwater Lake. Ursula attends the funeral. She tells Mr. Heerman, "When I gave up hope, then I began to live." He calls on her, wants to reassert their old relationship, but Ursula won't let that happen. He is nostalgic for their old life. She is not. He tells her, "You were the one I really cared about; you were my

41

equal"—the monstrous implication being that he could not marry a woman he could not dominate. He tells Ursula, "Frieda and Insley took care of my physical needs, you took care of my intellectual needs, and so you are far more significant." She slaps his face, tells him it's too bad he felt the need to separate his desires. She retires from her position at the school.

CUT TO:
Present day. Aunt Ursula is ninety-two. The principal's been dead for thirty years. His older boys moved away and have not been heard from. The baby, Bryce, died in Vietnam. Ursula's still in touch with the gentleman teacher, Merrill Fitz-Hugh. He lives in Key West. She walks across a wheat field—that same wheat field as earlier—toward the sunset.

DISSOLVE TO BLACK.

Michael, Shannon, and Dakotah Burns

A Family Gathering of Poetry

Sweet Potatoes
Michael Burns

When I was small, my father asked me before he left
for work one day if I would like, as he had taught me,
to dig some new potatoes out from the fall garden.
I did, carefully at first, with the short shovel,
making my way down to the first red skin,
then up and over my wrists with both of my hands.
I've still got this pale scar from the cut I took
from broken glass, to my finger. I stopped the bleeding.
I laid them in rows to show him when he came home.

I've made a spot in my back yard for tomatoes,
squash, green beans, ornamental red peppers.
And this year on a whim I decided to plant
sweet potatoes. Frost has fallen, and I'm so brave
I've gone this morning out to reap my rewards.
I spade the ground around the roots a little,
as if I were mapping some archaeological site,
but nothing shows. I take the shovel, plant my foot,
and the hell with it, I push until I hear
the cut of flesh, or something vegetable, and like it.

Oh, yes, I've found the scrawny, orange suckers
tunneling for China, like the mole, or diving
like a submarine under attack, and I go after them

with both hands again and dig for them, like runaways,
out of a rock and hard place. I swear I can feel the scar
in my finger throb. OK, you don't have to give me that,
but take time for a moment, as I must do, to imagine
my father standing here, in his work clothes and hat,
studying my crop. He laughs, but he's proud still
as I lay them down like trout, like ears of harvest corn,
like sweet-potatoes-not-worth-eating, in the yellow grass.
I must be about as old now as he was then.

Concerning Your Question
—for my daughter

Michael Burns

I didn't call you yesterday because I lost
my ear in the left lane of East Sunshine;
because my tongue stuck in the stump
of an old ache; because I told your brother
earlier in the day every good story I had
to tell, short of lying, and by night I knew
no lies worth your listening; because
I wanted to call you today to talk about
your birthday and bratwurst and beehive
hairdos and beyond-the-grave bubbled
breadfruit; and all of the weight of all
I had to say lay heavy on my chest
like a fat cat, in fact was probably
embodied in the actual fat of one
of at least five fat cats, and I fell forth
into a restless slumber, rumblings
and rain and thundering wind and limbs
coming down out of the crippled trees,
and you would not have wanted me
to wake and say such things to you,
worries and windings of loss and love
like a fresh-dressed kill, so I just stayed
asleep and snored I'm sure as if the world
went on ahead without me, which it did
not—I had a firm if tenuous hold, and hell
waited with its doors wide open
for some other happiness than mine.
Amen, said the congregation. The boy
is talking now. Fine foolishness. Amen

Being a Girl
Shannon Burns

I spilled cold coffee on every cushion
in the house, at the same moment, like a girl.
Dear Milk Chocolate Lion of Belgium, everyone
is my husband. Everyone cries on the telephone.
Everyone wants me to have a look at what this
bagel guillotine can do. I was just thinking,
me looking in your cabinets. You need soup
and apple butter. Apple butter comes in a glass
jar, and it'll break if you drop it, and then you're
down in the floor and you've got apple butter
in your hair again. And I was just thinking, I'm
just being such a girl, removing tough stains,
sitting Indian style and screaming, just being
a girl, blinking, biting, sleeping, coming over.

Brunt
Dakotah Burns

I remember where and why my chest is buried
in Hoosier Forest. A giant short-faced bear
found me low and sick and my face crowded
in soil singing through the roots that wind
and decline back to civilization: *goodbye, forever
and ever.* He slipped it off like so many slithery
evening clothes, pawed a clearing and lowered it
into mud. A bond can be made and was
between chest and man; we agreed to disagree,
we signed our annulment but I think of him
often, passing through Hoosier Forest on I-64 East,
entering and leaving, Chest staying, hibernating
in crust beneath glacial erratics. A phone call once
from the short-faced bear: *It will be winter soon,*
he said, *and I am thinking of your chest plate.*
*A freeze so unusual is coming that Hoosier will feel
a purple hue settle and sag on bark until it frowns
and sickles will crack the earth.* I knew that he knew
better than I, and I thought of my chest plate.
Years later rumors mounted, propagated mostly
by the short-faced bear, and I descended once more
beneath the canopy where no protection is offered
or desired, peered at the home of my Chest and spoke
over a cedar whistle to set the record straight: *Chest
in the snow, you are here and you have traded
my thermostat for liberty.* I breathed. *Word
on the street is you are starving and the roots
of your bed are faint and quaver.* No language
returned. I believed the sickles of the season
were kind when compared to abiding by the drag
of my memories and conclusions. I lay beside Chest then,
frozen, my cold-weather coat asleep over the pawed clearing.

Shannon Wooden

A Conversation with Kevin Brockmeier

In the early 1990's, Kevin Brockmeier and Shannon Wooden met in a creative writing class at Missouri State University. Since then, Brockmeier has established a national reputation as a fiction writer and essayist. Wooden, after completing a PhD at the University of North Carolina and teaching elsewhere, returns "home" this fall, joining the Missouri State University English Department as an assistant professor. In this conversation, Wooden (SRW) and Brockmeier (KB) begin by discussing his satiric essay, "I Remember 5 November 2008" (which follows in this volume) and continue with a wide-ranging discussion of memory, fiction, and music.

SRW: We're printing this conversation alongside an historically-rooted piece, about the 2008 presidential election. Can you give us some of your thought processes that went into writing it?

KB: The editor of a British magazine called *Five Dials* was gathering a set of imaginary essays written by various American writers. The assignment was to write a piece reflecting on the 2008 election from the perspective of a month or so after it had unfolded. This was in October, mind you—several weeks before Election Day—so none of us knew what would actually happen. My understanding is that the British newspaper *The Guardian* published a few of the pieces, including mine, on Election Day proper.

SRW: How, if at all, would you update it, given President Obama's first 100 days?

48

KB: Not at all. It was meant to stand as a sort of alternate-world period piece.

SRW: The political context is unusual for you, isn't it? I was a little surprised in the same way when Joyce Carol Oates put your story "The Ceiling" in the context of the 9/11 attack. It hadn't occurred to me to look for global-history antecedents to your writing—which is odd for me as a critic, now that I think of it. What was your feeling about that tie between your writing and current events?

KB: Of course I wrote "The Ceiling" well before 9/11. My real 9/11 story was actually a section of *The Truth About Celia*, a story called "The Telephone." I was working on that section of the book during September of 2001, and one of the conditions I had set for myself was that the incidents of the story would unfold within the actual historical context of the weeks I was writing it. And then, and then, well . . . the World Trade Center attacks happened when I was midway through the story. I felt unequipped to address the event in any substantive way so soon after it happened. So here's what I did: you'll find a moment in the story when Christopher's wife summons him into the living room to see something terrible on the television. Then there's a space break. And then he begins talking about the way people cope with loss by clinging to the objects that belonged to the dead and the missing. His own loss became everybody's loss. That's when 9/11 entered the story.

SRW: What about more personal history? You collect details more meticulously than anyone I've ever met. We've been friends for . . . what, eighteen years? I know you thought I was obsessed with lip gloss in those days . . .

KB: Seventeen, I think. I was a sophomore and you were a junior. But yes—the lip gloss. Before we knew each other, I used to see you in Pummill Hall or in the New Hall cafeteria, and you were always painting your lips with that long little brush. My friends and I used to have names for the various figures we would spot in the cafeteria. There was this one guy who was always wearing concert t-shirts: Rush, The Cure, Garth Brooks, Queen Latifah. It didn't make any sense to us—I mean, who likes every one of those performers? We called him The Enigma. Later we met someone who knew The Enigma. Apparently, he was the most mundane fellow you could imagine—nothing enigmatic about him at all. His name was Paul, I think. Anyway, we didn't have a name for you, but if we had, you would have been Lip Gloss Girl.

SRW: I'm not sure how to take that. Do you use biographical details about people you know as you design your characters? I have never been more thrilled in my life than to see myself in *The Brief History of the Dead*—I mean, when the main character mentioned that she had a friend with my name living in my state. That was close enough. I was reading in bed, and my husband Ken was down watching the news or something, and I went running downstairs yelling, "We're in this book! We're in this book!" I've had to show a hundred people. I was so excited. And still, I've been looking and looking for a character in your fiction who's obsessed with lip gloss, or at least someone who never appears to the narrator except when she's putting on lip gloss.

KB: I do use details about people I've known. Who knows? —Lip Gloss Girl might appear somewhere at some point. She would have made a good background figure in *The Brief History of the Dead*. The thing is, very rarely do I try to transport anyone I know fully onto the page. Usually I choose the smallest, most colorful pieces of my friends and acquaintances and blend them together with details I've drawn from my own life and from my mental life and from the lives of other people I've known or read about, and I try to—what?—to thread some kind of imaginative needle through the heart of the person I see taking shape before me, until I have something that feels like a whole human being.

SRW: So, have you ever used a piece of me?

KB: I'm sure I have, but I'd have to excavate my stories looking for it. Only in one instance—in my fiction (my essays are a different matter), have I tried to capture the whole character of someone I actually knew. That was in "Andrea Is Changing Her Name," which is by far the most autobiographical short story I've written, about a girl I knew when I was in high school.

SRW: Does she know?

KB: She does now, although I was very nervous about telling her. I wondered how she would feel about the fact that I was making use of her, or at least the person I imagined her to be, along with the person I used to be when I knew her and the relationship we had with each other, in order to write a short story. I felt when I was writing the story that in order to justify it I had to approach understanding her character and who she used to be and who I used to be in relation to her as generously as I possibly could, with as much honesty and as much love as I could muster up, and that maybe, if I allowed those impulses to guide me, everything would be all right. It was one of those stories that felt very dangerous to me as I was writing it. I found myself tiptoeing along from sentence to sentence, trying desperately not to make a single false step. In the end, I think the story was a success—it's one of my three favorites from the new collection. I published it in *Zoetrope*. Eventually, it was picked up for an anthology called *New Stories from the South*, and when that happened, I mailed her a copy of the anthology.

SRW: Did you talk to her at all about the story while you were writing it?

KB: No.

SRW: So she was surprised by it.

KB: She was. Later she said that she understood why I wrote it and what I was trying to express. And ultimately, I think she felt grateful for it . . . and thank God for that, because

51

the whole thing was really a sort of offering to her. God, I was crazy about her.

SRW: Are you still friends?

KB: Yes . . . though I don't see her very often. She's married and lives in Washington, D.C.

SRW: Hence the name-change of the story.

KB: That and something else. The story is ultimately about how easy it is to fail to honor the people we used to be, and how that failure is a disservice to our past selves, yes, but also to the people who loved us back then and continue to love us. In other words, you'd damn well better love the person you used to be, because I sure do.

SRW: Do you remember how you and I met? I don't remember if we were friends before that poetry class we took together or if we became friends in there, but I do remember a few details from those days. Your "Einstein at Breakfast" is still one of my favorite poems.

KB: All I remember about that poem is the last line: "Oy vey. I should have been a plumber" (which—minus the "oy vey"—are supposed to have been Einstein's real last words).

SRW: My most vivid memory is of the first line: "Make it your damn self." Can't tell you how many times I've muttered that to myself over the years.

KB: Every so often, someone will come to me with a much clearer memory of something I wrote than I have. Not long ago, I ran across a girl from my high school creative writing class—she showed up at a reading I gave—who told me how much she had liked a prose-poem I wrote for our class. It was about lemmings, apparently. The title was "Cute, Small, Fuzzy." Ugh. But yes, we met the first semester of my sophomore—your junior—year, when I started working at the University Writing Center and we took Michael Burns's poetry workshop together. "Hey, it's Lip Gloss Girl!" I must have thought to myself. I do remember—this would have been toward the end of that same school year—that I spotted you cutting through the lobby of my dorm building, and suddenly I had this flash of you as you must have been when you were a little girl. Something about your stride or the way you were carrying your books, I don't know. Anyway, at the time, I had this notion that you couldn't really know an adult until you had some sharp revelatory glimpse of the child inside them, and you couldn't really know a child until you had some sharp revelatory glimpse of the adult inside them. So you probably weren't aware of this, but as far as I was concerned, that was when we really became friends.

SRW: I was probably tripping over something. Apparently I was not a very graceful little thing. I wonder sometimes when I'm reading your stories—about and for children, and in the voice of parents or caretakers—if I'm seeing you as a child. It's odd to me, as a parent, how often I think I see you as a parent. I don't know how you do that without having had children. But you did work in day care, didn't you? What did that experience do for you? Do you think anyone has ever looked at you . . . shall I say, *askance*, because of the story, "These Hands"?

KB: I hope not, but who can say? "These Hands" came about because I wanted to write a story in which a man who wasn't crazy and wasn't malign fell in love with a child. In some ways it was a take on the life of the Reverend Charles Dodgson, aka Lewis Carroll—thus the names of the characters: Lewis and Caroline. As for the years I spent working at the nursery school, they were tremendously important to me, easily one of the best things I've done with my life. I used to make up stories for the kids—a different one every day about them and their wild adventures. I can tell you that I wouldn't have begun writing children's fiction if it weren't for the fact that I missed those particular kids and wanted to find a way to keep telling them stories. My first kids' book, *City of Names*, is actually dedicated to them.

SRW: I understand this is your first interview with someone you have been friends with for a long time. Anything particular you'd like to talk to me about, maybe something you haven't had an opportunity to talk about in previous interviews?

KB: Well, there *is* a glaring hole in the history of my interviews: not a single question about M——.

SRW: And I never would have thought to ask, either. Anything in particular you have to say about M——?

KB: Well . . . no. Not really. Boy, that question was a dud, wasn't it?

SRW: Thinking about M—— just reminds me what I bitch I could be in those days.

KB: Were you a bitch to M——?

SRW: Yeah, I guess so. I was probably kind of a bitch to a lot of people—I vaguely remember a fair amount of drama. M—— had a crush on Brian the Librarian, with whom I was carrying on something of a flirtation . . . okay, stalking, whatever. I suppose I should have backed off when I knew she liked him, but I didn't. As it turned out, he wasn't really that into either of us, but I guess I messed up her chance.

KB: I don't remember Brian the Librarian.

SRW: God, I had a devastating crush. A crushing crush. He was cute, smart, read books . . . and he had this amazing long hair. Lord. And, of course, he wasn't into me, which was about the most attractive thing in the world.

KB: Yeah, I do remember you complaining about all the guys that were into you.

SRW: See? Wasn't I a bitch?

KB: I didn't see you that way. The thing is, you were lovely. I remember very distinctly a conversation we had in the Writing Center one day. Yet another friend-and-only-a-friend had developed a crush on you, and you wanted to know why this kept happening. I said, "I can tell you exactly why that is. Three things: (1) You're attractive. (2) You actually listen to people when they're talking to you. (3) You touch people casually. People interpret that as, she's crazy about me."

SRW: I'm sorry . . . did you say something? I was putting on lip gloss.

KB: Don't mind me. I'm just touching up my mascara. But another Writing Center conversation I remember is when you and Stefani Marion were talking about the movie *Interview with the Vampire* and complaining that Tom Cruise looked "thin-lipped and beaky." My response was to gesture at myself and say, "What's wrong with thin-lipped and beaky?" That went over big.

SRW: The earliest things I remember about our friendship, I think, are those eccentric and amazing mix cassette tapes you made. I still have some of them, though for years I haven't owned anything I could play them on. I have always wanted to know whether you see compilations like that as having a kind of narrative. I mean, do you use them to communicate something to the person that you're making them for?

KB: It depends on the person. I definitely made mix tapes—and later CDs—that were nothing but message. Usually, though, there were four or five songs interspersed in the mix that actually expressed what I wanted to say. The rest were simply songs I thought the person would enjoy. Or songs that had come up in conversation. Or songs that contained references to features of our shared experience. Or songs I saw as an expression of my own character. In your case, that first tape would have been a "Hi, I'm getting to know you, and here are some songs I like, and maybe you'll like some of them, too" mix. The later tapes would have been more personal. I remember making one for you during the unhappiest phase of your first marriage that had a lot of songs about people in unhappy marriages.

SRW: Oh, God. I think I blocked that. John Gorka was on there, I think . . . and maybe Dar Williams's "February"? I learned to play that on my guitar, right about then—I think

I learned to play the guitar just so I could play that song as some kind of therapy. I'd play and sing and cry—it was kind of nuts, but surprisingly effective. Do you have any songs that stand out like that in your life—personal anthems or soundtracks of a moment?

KB: Absolutely I do. Age ten: "Always Something There to Remind Me" by Naked Eyes. The first semester of my freshman year of college: "Sometimes It Snows in April" by Prince. Age twenty, the year I spent in Ireland: "I Love the World" by New Model Army. My first year of graduate school: "Further and Further Away" by Cheryl Wheeler. Age 25: "Sweet Thing" by Van Morrison. The awful canoe trip I took down the Buffalo: "My Life" by Iris DeMent. These days it would be anything, anything at all, by Susanna and the Magical Orchestra. I still like all these songs, but how about this? Age thirteen, embarrassingly: "Nothing's Gonna Change My Love for You" by Glenn Medeiros. There you go: the sad, sticky heart of young Kevin Brockmeier. I should make you a mix of the songs I loved at age thirteen, and that's what I can call it: "The Sad, Sticky Heart of Young Kevin Brockmeier."

SRW: Even if I could remember back to the songs that reflected my heart at thirteen, I don't think I'd want to. I do have a very painful memory involving "Purple Rain" and my sixteenth birthday. But your mix tapes had lives of their own. Many of the artists that were on tapes you made for me I ended up liking a lot in other contexts as well, and I liked a lot of their other songs . . . but then some of them didn't hold up in any context other than the one in which they originally appeared to me. So, Alison Moyet, yes, I ended up liking her a lot.

KB: She's still releasing music, you know. A couple of the CDs she's put out recently are as good as anything she's done: *Hometime* and *Voice*. *Voice* is mostly standards: "Windmills of Your Mind," "Cry Me a River."

SRW: But Elton and Betty White? That song about oral sex? What was up with that?

KB: It's funny you should mention that—because I just wrote a long article about Elton and Betty White for the Southern Music Issue of *The Oxford American*. I wrote another one for them, about Iris DeMent and my journey down the Buffalo, a year or so ago. Those two pieces, I think, are actually some of the best writing I've done recently. The Elton and Betty White essay is about their lives and their music and the meaning they had for me personally when I was growing up in Little Rock in the 1980's. When I first became aware of them, Betty was a short, eccentric white woman in her late sixties, and Elton was a tall, lanky black man in his mid-thirties. And they were a couple, with thirty years separating them. And they'd walk around Little Rock in sombreros and very skimpy swimwear, playing ukuleles and singing songs about their sex life, which was an unusual sight at the time, to say the least. Unusual and wonderful. I always felt—I had a strangely intimate relationship with them and their music. I even interviewed them once in high school for a research paper I wrote: it was supposed to be on some aspect of Arkansas culture, and the aspect I chose was Elton and Betty White. They've meant a lot to me. Read the essay, and I think you'll understand why. I'd be curious to hear what you think.

SRW: That's wonderful. I will! I'm glad I brought them up—I didn't expect such a response!

KB: I've got a folder that contains all my old mix lists.

SRW: I'm not at all surprised you have that. You are an unbelievable archivist.

KB: I'm trying to find the Shannon lists.

SRW: The ones I still have are "Against Regret," and one that's a two-tape collection called "The Beach" and "The Sea."

KB: Let's see. I just found the one with the Elton & Betty White songs and the Alison Moyet. And "Come On, Eileen," which I still love. And "Last Chance Waltz," which breaks my heart. And a cover of "Losing My Religion" by a band called Tesco Vee's Hate Police. And a song called "Shut Up," by NY Style. I have no idea what that is. Oh, and there, by god, is a tape for M——!

SRW: I knew we'd work her in somehow! I want to ask you about the lists that you keep. I know you do, what, top 50? Music, books . . .

KB: Yes, my 50 favorite books, short stories, movies, albums, songs, children's books—which I put together for a children's fiction workshop I just taught at the Iowa Writers' Workshop. And then I keep an ongoing list of my 50 least favorite books, although I've never shared that one with anybody. It would just make people angry.

SRW: Right, of course, though I'd love to see it. Do you keep the old lists when you update one? Do you have a folder or something that you keep them in?

KB: No, though I imagine there are copies lingering in various desk drawers around the country. I give them out at readings—the lists, not the drawers—so I'm sure they're available somewhere.

SRW: Do you think that your lists are interpretable? I mean, do you think somebody could look at your lists and understand something about you, other than your tastes?

KB: Well, I think my tastes are an important part of who I am. I mean, I spend the majority of my life reading books. That's how I fill my time. It's how I fill my mind. That and conversing with friends, reminiscing about my own life, speculating about various things. And writing, of course. I don't know—it feels as if whenever I revise one of these lists, I'm capturing a new version of my personality. And then, over time, I change, and the list becomes outdated, so I have to reconsider it. I have to include some wonderful new book I've read, or I reevaluate a book that seems less essential to me than it used to.

SRW: Has anything ever made it from the bad list to the good list?

KB: Oh, no no no. That would be quite a leap. The books on the bad list are there for a reason. But there have been books that didn't mean much to me one way or the other, or books that kept climbing in my estimation as I thought about them, that have later clawed their way onto the 50 Favorites list.

SRW: Do you watch television?

KB: I do, but not much. My television is a 1976 Curtis Mathes that I inherited from my stepfather. It's a color TV, but it's from an early enough era of the technology that it's got one of those little color blocks beneath the dial—the red, blue, and green square. It failed to accompany the rest of the world through the digital revolution last week, though, so I guess I'm without a TV right now. But, yeah, usually there are a couple of programs I like to keep up with. Lately it's been the American version of *The Office*. I like to watch Letterman or Leno—or O'Brien now, I guess—for half an hour or so before I go to bed.

SRW: But it's not on a par with what you refer to as "how you fill your mind."

KB: No, it's not. There have been a few TV shows that have been really important to me, and I know there are a lot of really good shows out there right now on cable, too. I just haven't had the opportunity to see them. I want to catch up with some of them eventually on DVD. But I think the only television show that is as meaningful to me as my favorite books and albums and movies is *Freaks and Geeks* ... which I think was a perfect 18-episode series. It never took a misstep, and it offered a much deeper exploration of its characters than most other TV shows. And it happens to be about the early-80s. Though all the characters are a little bit older than I was at the time, it's still a time period that resonates with me.

SRW: Ah, the eighties. Did you enjoy high school?

KB: I did. I loved high school. Junior high was terrible. Elementary school was great, for the most part. It seemed to take up centuries of my life, but that was okay—those were the best centuries of my life. Junior high, though, was about as bad as it could be. My high school was a performing arts magnet. And it was great. I didn't want to leave when it was over. It was very hard for me. I had a large network of friends—close friends. They all meant so much to me and the idea that we were going to be scattering across the United States—"spreading our souls across the world"—it was just really hard for me. So I wasn't happy to be going to SMSU initially.

SRW: Wow. Nothing could be further from my experience with high school. Your story gives me hope for my own children. My experience—well, I can't even remember elementary school. We moved. I think I thrived in junior high because things started to get the tiniest bit challenging but it was before all the emotional drama started. I was delighted to get to college—which, despite all *its* drama, was an easier place for me to be comfortable.

KB: I suppose that junior high was for me more like high school was for you. I got to leave the emotional drama behind when I went to high school. And suddenly it was as if . . . I don't want to overstate things, but it was a wonderful environment, and also I was simply very good at being a student. And that's where my social life was rooted. I got to know people first in the classroom, and then I could carry my classroom self into the rest of my life. And because I was very comfortable with my classroom self it made my social life a lot easier. And then I went to college, and there were people I got to know in the classroom, yes, but I wasn't spending the entire day together with them in the same building. You had to make friends in some other way, to establish your character through . . . well, what every other person in the world would consider normal, human interaction. But it was much easier for me to do it my old, neurotic, peculiarly adjusted way.

SRW: I have a feeling you're a very self-aware person, someone who spends a lot of time thinking about your thinking.

KB: I think that's true. Or at least I *think* I think that's true. Ba-dum. Of course, I've had insomnia over the past few years, and that may be a product of thinking *too* much about my thinking.

SRW: Don't take this the wrong way—I mean it as praise: I have always suspected that you think more like a critic than other people I know who are creative writers . . . and I think most of the people I know who are creative writers would take offense at such a statement, because they attribute their writing ability almost exclusively to inspiration and artistry—to something they see as categorically different from critical or analytical writing—rather than a more deliberate or thoughtful craftsmanship.

KB: I know what you mean. I think inspiration is certainly an important part of what it means to write fiction, but a relatively small part. The actual work of writing is trying to craft one good sentence after another, and unless you can cast a critical eye on a sentence, you'll never produce a story of real value. I think the inspiration, the artistry, takes place in the background of my work while I'm concentrating on the craft. In other words, I'll spend ages and ages on a sentence, and by the time I've shaped it into a form I can live with, my mind has already suggested to me where the story should go next.

SRW: I certainly don't mean for the word "craftsmanship" to suggest "workmanlike." Your writing is obviously very imaginative and playful—amazingly so. What do you find are the differences for you, in process, between writing for kids and writing for adults?

KB: Several things. One is that I find it much easier to write for children. The reason for that, I think, is that the children's fiction I write is in the first person, from the point of view of a clever, slightly odd little boy, somewhere between the ages of 10 and 13, and that little boy is an awful lot like I was at that age. So basically I'm trying to capture what I think was my natural speaking voice back then, which is a voice that lingers somewhere in the back of my head anyway, and put it on the page. If I can find a way to access that voice, the sentences come more naturally to me than they usually do when I'm trying to write for adults.

SRW: When you write for adults, you do a lot of different voices, many of which are not like you autobiographically at all.

KB: I think that's true. Occasionally there will be stories that pick up something of what I think of as my interior speaking voice, and maybe even some of the best stories do this: "A Fable With Slips of White Paper Spilling from the Pockets," "The View from the Seventh Layer." But they don't mimic the way I actually sound in conversation. Nobody who knows me would read them and feel as if they were talking to me. Aside from that, one of the things I've discovered is that there's a difference between fiction that moves forward paragraph by paragraph and fiction that moves forward sentence by sentence. When I'm writing for adults, the unit of meaning that carries my stories forward is the sentence, and when I'm writing for children it's the paragraph. I don't know why this is the case, but it is. And then my children's fiction is intended to be funny. There are moments of humor in my adult fiction, as well, but it's not as joke-riddled, as filled with puns and gags and things like that, as my children's fiction.

SRW: Do you go through a conscious process—a kind of method acting or something—to become a character that is, say, much older than you, or female? I remember being really impressed with *Celia*, all those years ago, because I couldn't imagine how you could represent so well what it felt and sounded like to be a father, to be a grieving father of a lost child—all these experiences you hadn't had that you seemed to capture exquisitely.

KB: Well, thank you. What I can say is that I felt I understood, for whatever reason, the emotional architecture of that character. I don't know why. I just did. One way in which *The Truth About Celia* differs from all the other fiction I've written is that it's presented through the prism of another writer. My original title for the book was *The Celia Stories by Christopher Brooks: A novel by Kevin Brockmeier*. The idea is that all these stories are being presented through the impulses of this other writer. So, really, what I felt like I was doing when I wrote that book was role-playing. I was trying to inhabit the mind of this other writer, Christopher Brooks, and then let *him* experiment with inhabiting the minds of all the other people who flesh out the novel, like his daughter and his wife. I found a freedom in allowing myself to say, "These are stories written by some other person." What I did was just follow the impulses of that other writer.

SRW: That doesn't sound like something teachable.

KB: Well, remember I was once a theater major in college, along with a creative writing and philosophy major. I became more and more interested in writing as the semesters passed and I became less and less interested in theater—at least, less and less interested in exposing myself physically to other people. (And by "exposing myself," I don't mean what *you* think I mean. I'm still very interested in *that*. Just ask the Arkansas State Police.) Seriously, though, if there's one thing that has most helped me inhabit the minds, if not the bodies, of other people—one thing aside from reading book after book after book—that's probably it.

SRW: I've thought a number of times about your decision to major in philosophy as training for a creative writer, but

I've never until this minute thought about the contribution theater must have made.

KB: Well, when I studied acting, I realized very quickly that I had so little awareness of what I was doing with my own body that I was totally unable to bring an awareness to myself of what it would be like to inhabit someone else's body. I was completely inept when it came to *embodying* another character. I couldn't do it. But I wasn't too bad when it came to inhabiting the *consciousness* of another character. It wasn't the sort of thing I could employ with any ease on the stage, but it was something I could bring to the page.

SRW: So, to "embody" Christopher's grief at the loss of his child . . .

KB: Well I wrote *The Truth About Celia* treating each section as a self-contained short story. I didn't feel that I had to write it in order from the beginning to the end, as I would a typical novel. The first section I wrote was actually the last section of the book, which is called "Love is a Chain, Hope is a Weed." I didn't know it was going to be part of a novel at the time. I was treating it as an independent short story. But when I finished the story, I had all these other ideas about the events in question—the disappearance of a daughter, the dissolution of a marriage—and how a father and a husband would go about dealing with them. And eventually that produced a novel. I think the reason I was so engaged by all those events and felt I could speak with some authority about them was that it was a way of talking about certain aspects of my own life that I've been grappling with. It's a book about loss, and about using the imagination and the memory as a way of retaining those things you've been forced to abandon. There's a grief that comes along with growing older, and leaving certain things, certain people, behind, and divesting yourself of all the tiny details of the life you used to lead. That's what it's like for me, at least. This feeling is right at the center of my experience of the world, and I suspect it contributed greatly to the emotional undercurrent of the book.

SRW: Nicely said. I think I feel that sense of loss more acutely now that my kids grow older every day. I don't think I ever meditated on my own history that much, but theirs, definitely.

KB: I'm trying to find another one of your playlists . . . You should see these. Long lists of songs with question marks and asterisks beside them. Songs to include and songs to discard. Songs to begin a side and songs to end one. Some of them are even color coded with highlighter pens. I had these intricate methods of putting a mix together . . . "I'm In Love With Your Behind . . ."

SRW: Why, thank you.

KB: You're welcome! Any time, toots!

SRW: Whose was "I'm In Love With Your Behind?"

KB: Elton White.

SRW: Of course.

KB: What I'm looking for—I remember there was a Meryn Cadell song called "Being in Love," and I used to sing it all the time, which irritated you because it's kind of crass, so I put it on a mix tape for you and then *you* were singing it all the time. Do you remember? "Being in love really sucks . . . babies cost a lot of money . . ."

SRW: Oh, of course! "Please don't make me f—" . . . Oops! Can't sing that line—my son's in the room! The one that talks! Wow. I would love to listen those again.

KB: Well, I could put most of them back together, but there are a few songs I don't even remember.

SRW: We could google them. Do you ever google yourself?

KB: Never. Never never never. Not once. I never look myself up online, never read any reviews.

SRW: You've never read any of your reviews?

KB: Not a one.

SRW: Really? Well, they really like you.

KB: Thanks, and that's good to hear. I just don't want to fill my head with all that stuff. Good or bad, I think it would be nothing but damaging. Allowing yourself to be defined by what other people have had to say about you—I think my writing would be worse, my life would be worse, everything would be worse.

SRW: Then I think you've made a good decision. Hey, one of these days, send me another music mix, okay?

Kevin Brockmeier

I Remember 5 November 2008

As late as November the 3rd, no one could have imagined that the election would culminate the way it did. Certainly I couldn't.

After all, who would have guessed that the worst accusations lobbied against John McCain by Barack Obama's most fervent supporters, and against Barack Obama by John McCain's, would turn out to be true? That Barack Obama was indeed a covert Muslim terrorist—and also, simultaneously, a radical Black Christian—whose true agenda was to disenfranchise white Americans, institute a broad-based socialist agenda of government hand-outs and immense taxation, then hand the whole nation over to the terrorists and retire to an island in the Caribbean? That John McCain was in fact a doddering old fool—and also, simultaneously, a vicious ultra-conservative mastermind— whose actual goal was to deprive middle-class Americans of health care, job opportunities, and all their hard-earned social freedoms before dying a year into office and allowing Sarah Palin to assume the mantle of power, appointing Dick Cheney her Vice President and puppet-master? And that it would all come to light on the afternoon before election day, in a fashion so conspicuous and indisputable?

It was a dispiriting turn of events, to say the least.

Of course most Americans, horrified by the choice with which they suddenly had been presented—a terrorist on one ticket and a dictator on the other—and unable to fathom voting for the Libertarians or (God forbid) the Greens, chose to stay home from the polls on November the 4th. But as for the rest of us, and I number myself among them, what were we to do? In the privacy of the voting booth, how were we to make our decision?

I'm sure you'll recall the chaos of election night, as poll workers across the nation counted by hand the tens of millions of write-in candidates whose names marked our ballots. It was several weeks before every vote was recorded and the tabulations checked and rechecked.

As the whole world now knows, the winner, by some ten-thousand ballots, was America's most beloved movie personality, Tom Hanks. Mr. Hanks is neither a radical Black Christian Muslim terrorist nor a near-dead senile ultra-conservative, but a patriot. He has announced that he is prepared to accept the responsibilities of high command and is scheduled to be inaugurated on January the 20th, which according to *Entertainment Weekly* should give him just enough time to finish his voice-over work for *Toy Story 3* before assuming the duties of office.

We are all wondering who he will name as his Vice President. I'm rooting for Julia Roberts. Julia Roberts or maybe Will Smith. I'll be happy either way.

In any case, I am certain Mr. Hanks will get the economy, the housing crisis, and that nasty business in the Middle East straightened out in no time. I, for one, am looking forward to four years of peace, prosperity, and delightful Pixar productions, the kind with those hysterical fake out-takes at the end—you know the ones I mean. I am filled with hope for the future.

Billy Clem

Some Confirmation: A Gay Man Comes of Age in the Missouri Ozarks

In spite of illness, in spite of the arch-enemy sorrow, one *can* remain alive long past the usual date of disintegration if one is unafraid of change, insatiable in intellectual curiosity, interested in big things, happy in small ways. In the course of sorting and setting down my memories I have learned that these advantages are usually independent of one's merits . . . .

—Edith Wharton

I am the son of two white U.S. (American) citizens both born in the mid-twentieth century to poor and working class families. My mother comes from near total Irish ancestry out of working-class Chicago. Most of the men were cops; her grandfather, father, and many, many uncles and cousins patrolled the streets for years (my grandfather guarded the first Mayor Daley, the picture of which still hangs in my Mom's home). The women—those very few who received any higher education, an aunt, one sister—were teachers. (Perhaps there is a nurse somewhere)? The other women were, of course, "homemakers." Everybody else in the family got whatever jobs were available, usually "unskilled," meaning undervalued, low-paid labor. This family, the O'Mearas, after decades of struggle, moved out of the Irish-American ghettos into small, all-white working class neighborhoods. Catholics, of course, they eventually assimilated thoroughly and became what people here in the U.S. would call politically conservative; elsewhere, generally fascist, believing in a rather narrow idea of what constitutes humanity—Catholic, white, male, heterosexual, fully abled and aspiring to middle-class respectability. They are a tough-love family, at least, but they maintain ties to one another pretty well; they come together often for christenings, birthday parties, weddings, and funerals. They can put away their beer, and, as Southside Irish, they love the Chicago White Sox, and, of course, *da Bears*. When I've had the chance to reconnect with this extended family from my mother's side, I find that they are very kind, offering lots of food and their political opinions freely. One can imagine our conversations short and visits infrequent. And the few of us who are a bit different from the standard congregate and smile.

My father's family is mostly Irish, with some Scottish and Cherokee, and there are rumors of African ancestry, though I am the only one willing to discuss or inquire into this aspect. They are very poor, white southerners from rural Tennessee. Bootleggers during prohibition, they can still get you moonshine if you need it. All laborers at one point, a few of the Clems or their familial off-shoots have moved into management positions in what still passes as "blue-collar" labor: construction and/or plumbing. Generous and kind people if you're family, or just exceedingly friendly if you're not, they will feed you all day long. And it's delicious, southern cooking that, for one with Crohn's disease (*c'est moi*) or any other ailment, can lead rather quickly to a stomach ache that, when reflected upon, was worth the trouble. And the accent is truly lovely. I hardly ever see my father's family (distance, time, and sadly, on all our parts, interest?) but when I hear an east-Tennessee/northern-Georgia accent (think of hearing Loretta Lynn's beautiful voice) I hear my dad and his family immediately. There is something lovely there.

My parents, Catherine and Billy, met in the early 1970s and after just a few months of romance, married against her white, Catholic, middle-class-aspiring family's ideas of appropriate marriage. No doubt, this marrying down, or at least laterally, appealed to her in some way. It appealed to him, too, I think. His non-Catholic upbringing, frank talk, and strange accent undid her family who could not tolerate the idea that one of their own would marry an un(der)educated laborer from the U.S. South. His family was somewhat better about the marriage; his mother already gone, his sisters embraced the beautiful, young, "Northern" bride—albeit from a distance of some 500 miles. They made a sort of mixed-marriage, and were, emotionally and financially, on their own.

Their relationship, I believe, was strained at the beginning. A fast marriage, no money, and few prospects for good jobs (he had little high school and she just got through the Chicago public school system of the 1960s with its low standards and racist and sexist problems), money was always scarce. Her intolerant family and his far away didn't help. And after becoming pregnant rather quickly, my Mom delivered a baby a year into the marriage who, tragically, died immediately. It seems, from piecing together the story over many years, from hearing my Mom's reflections on this time, that she had little or no support in grieving properly for her lost baby, her first child, and for herself. Her pain is unfathomable to me because it is so profound; I understand it but cannot imagine it thoroughly. My Dad's pain is palpable, though I couldn't swear to it as he and I don't share our feelings and needs as she and I do. (Certainly, among U.S. men, sharing feelings isn't always acceptable, and I venture to believe that this is very much the case among poor and working-class men, for shame in capitalism and training in maleness produce feelings of unwanted weakness; though not in all instances, this is certainly the case among many I know). As a result, sometime later, they tried pregnancy again. They decided that if this one took, they'd go on. And so, sometime later, in late 1973, I was born.

With one child now, a coveted boy, their lives seemed to improve. Dad had completed night school to be a truck driver and was now driving for Zenith, and though this job required him to be gone six of seven days each week, it paid well. Mom was now home full-time, no longer working at Burger King where she had been since high school, and enjoyed to some degree staying home with her new baby. It is, I believe, important for me to acknowledge that while she had a child and enjoyed some aspects of motherhood, she missed very much the opportunities that come with working away from home. And though the separations from each other and the worlds they knew were difficult for both of them, more so for her I think as she alone cared full-time for an infant, these were decent days financially. Of course, I have no direct memory of this time, but I imagine them (from seeing the pictures and hearing the stories) as "fairly good days." A young, good-looking couple, a cute baby with blond hair and blue eyes, and enough money to pay bills and have things make for a decent picture, something American-dream like.

Things began to change when more children came. Though more than happy to have more children, all beautiful and "healthy," the young couple found that money became much tighter with more mouths to feed. Identical twin girls—a surprise at the delivery that more than one baby had come—Catherine and Elizabeth were born in 1975. My Mom became the envy of her family and friends because twins are always something bigger and better. But, with Dad on the road all the time, Mom had no one to help her with three children—a two-year old and infant twins. Of course, she became depressed and anxious, for who would not under such stress? She found, I believe, little or no sympathy (and certainly no help) from her family, neighbors, and friends. In fact, recently, my Mom shared with me that, some months after the twins were born, she asked one of her sisters why she (my Mom) cried all the time and felt terrible. The sister replied that all women felt this way after children were born.

72

And that was the end of the conversation. She had no one to whom she could ask these important questions, no where to go in a time of dire need, no one with whom to cry. And, as one can imagine, the feminist movement had not quite made it to South-side white Irish Chicago and allowed women to seek help from each other. In essence, she sucked it up and did what she could, which, I believe, became a soul-destroying existence. It is little wonder to me now that during my childhood her temper could be short; his always was, too, after, no doubt, grueling driving and the delivering of TVs. This is, probably, one source of my chronic anxiety: fearing that I'm saying the wrong thing or bothering someone, I have always become nervous when approaching any new situation, even with familiar people.

Two more babies came quickly: Samantha in 1977, and Hollis (Geno) in 1980. Because the money was tight (and tighter all the time—this was the late 70s and early 80s with inflation and backlash from anti-civil rights people), Dad was working all the time; with no outside help available, Mom decided the family was big enough. Five little mouths to feed, clothe, and educate was more than plenty—no doubt, it was too much. And though I am very uncomfortable writing this, and though it has taken me years to come to terms with this, I must admit that my parents' drinking became serious. They maintained their jobs, of course, but along with drinking, as anyone growing up around alcoholism can attest, comes abuse and neglect. Though party nights could be fun for us—lots of soda (pop as it's called in Chicago) and potato chips, late nights of TV, friends sleeping over, and adults sometimes fawning over you—these parties often gave me, as a young boy, a feeling of despondency. I felt lost, afraid, and unsettled. This disorder, or unproductive anarchy, that comes with such drinking parties and loud music, with adults fighting or laughing or loving uncontrollably, with staying up rather late and waking up to hung-over, grumpy parents, made me feel unmoored, made me want stability, order, and permanence. So, as a young boy, I searched without knowing it for the people and the place where I would find that stability, order, and permanence: I found school, and, fortunately for me, therein I flourished.

I loved school as a young boy—absolutely and unconditionally. I loved to read and write, and did so all the time, even when I should have been doing something else. And, in general, I was a good student; eager and bright, I was liked by the teachers and earned good grades. Certainly I had friends with whom I played on the playground during recess, but nothing mattered more than being in the classroom doing schoolwork. I loved worksheets and textbooks and all the good marks I received—all this is good practice indeed for a teacher-to-be. In fact, I loved school so much that I could not bear to be absent. A now-funny story still circulates about my refusing to stay home when sick. In first grade, each student had the opportunity to lead the "Pledge of Allegiance" and conduct some patriotic song by waving his or her right hand in a triangle while standing in front of the class. My turn came the day I was sick with a cold. My parents told me that I could not go to school. I cried and complained, and they sent me back to bed. So, while they sat in the kitchen drinking coffee, I dressed and walked myself to school—as a six year old in a large city. This, of course, became something of a capital offense, for walking to school alone was totally forbidden—safety, I'm sure. I can still only imagine the panic they must have felt when they went into my room and did not find me sick in bed, still complaining of the injustice of being made to stay home on what was the most important day of my life thus far! And how they knew to look for me at school makes me laugh aloud today; they knew me well! So, there I was at my desk hearing Mrs. Brown say, "Billy, today is your day to lead us. . . ." when I saw my Dad and the school counselor at the classroom door. Immediately, I burst into tears and yelled out how much I wanted to stay at school and lead the class today! Mrs. Brown helped me to gather my stuff and led me to the door. Beyond this, I have no memory of the event, but my parents do and still talk about it: how angry and frightened they were at first and then how perplexed that one of their own was such a nerd so early in life! This illustrates, I think, my early devotion to all things school. This devotion continued even with the devastating move from Chicago to rural southwest Missouri that my family had to make because of my Dad's job's relocation.

This move, coming when I was not quite nine years old, at the end of third grade, was a difficult adjustment for all of us. Rural southwest Missouri is nothing like Southside Chicago, to say the least. The only characteristic they share is the same language, in a much different accent. The move devastated my Mother who was moving from all she knew and loved: her parents, friends, and the (great) city of Chicago. She had lived in this community her entire life and thought of herself as a member of a working-class culture that, whatever its problems, was comfortable in many ways: neighbors could sometimes be depended upon in an emergency, and the sharing of some resources was a given; these hallmarks of working-class communities did not/do not exist in this new place in Misery, what we came to call our new state. Leaving all this for a small town in Missouri would be/was miserable for her. But my Father was fine with it. He had moved often and traveled constantly, so this wouldn't be too much of a change; furthermore, he'd be moving back to the South—albeit a different region but still the South. And it seems that he had won the silent contest with his father-in-law: my mother and these kids would be entirely dependent upon him (my Dad) alone. And he was now a landowner. My siblings, so small and under six years old, seemed fine with it. I hated the idea of this move and its completion. I remember vividly my Mom's coming into my bedroom to tell me that we were going to live in Marshfield, Missouri. I couldn't believe it and begged her not to make us go; all I could picture was the scenery in *Little House on the Prairie*: a badly-leaning home and a one-room schoolhouse with bitchy Nellie Olsen ordering us all around! Of course, Marshfield and its school were not the world of Laura Ingalls Wilder, mercifully, but it was, and still is, a place about which I am at best ambivalent because of its right-wing, fundamentalist Christian ideology and its open, hostile racism, sexism, classism, heterosexism, ableism, and ageism. But the landscape, the Ozark Mountains and valleys, the old winding roads, the communities of Amish peoples, is incomparable. And some of its nearly all-white-population were/could be kind and caring—especially the teachers (no surprise). It is, at least, an interesting place, one full of contradictions for someone like me.

Their funny accents, their not taking to me because I was not like anything they knew, and my isolation were both a source of pain and wonder to me, from as early as fourth grade. It was clear immediately that my family was not middle-class in a town that valued conservative, white, Protestant values of obedience to a vengeful, Old Testament God, immaculate lawns, small families, and the pretensions of upward mobility through capitalist connections. This petite-bourgeois was quite content with its sterility and unquestioned hostility to outsiders. And we were loud, strange, and poor. We had a nice house at the edge of town (purchased and financed with inheritance money from one of my Mom's "maiden" aunts—a home that has been foreclosed upon, now as I write, by a bank after 25 years of payments due to what we hear in the news media is a "recent mortgage crisis"), but my parents drank beer and smoked cigarettes outside by our pool, and we ran around, as one of my classmates' mother's said to him, as "unsupervised" children. (This remark continues to be a source of much amusement). My truck-driver father cursed often and made fun of other people openly. My Mom was constantly asked if she knew Al Capone. And money issues abounded; there was never enough for everything, and the constant worry over paying the bills, losing or not losing the house, having another car repossessed, was ever present. And while my siblings seemed to be fine, most of the kids who pronounced the word "the" as "thee" said I ran like a girl and that I was funny looking because my dark eyebrows didn't match my blond hair. Over time, I found that I had neither aptitude for nor interest in the things that most (but not all, to be honest) of the other boys valued: sports, hunting, money, and objectifying and harassing (hating but wanting) girls. Moving from elementary school through junior high school, puberty, on into high school, and realizing that I had feelings and ideas not universally shared but openly denigrated—finding sports boring, guns frightening, money pointless if not divisive, and girls to be equals and friends and boys to be those for whom I had sexual feelings—forced me to try to make myself invulnerable to a hostile world, to build an invisible wall that no one could penetrate. (Frighteningly, I thought this worked for a long time). Realizing that what I heard at school, in the culture, and at home about myself and other people—that African Americans were criminals, Asians evil geniuses, gays sick and wrong, the disabled an unwanted and unnecessary burden, the poor destitute because of laziness, women stupid and pliant—contradicted everything I knew, felt, and believed. It contradicted my entire existence, and I could not countenance it: it made no sense to me ever to be self-hating and/or to hate others who had never wronged me. Naturally I have always been disposed to like people, to get along if not with genuine affection at least with civility. But I was forced, because I could not and would not participate, financially or emotionally, in the activities that others participated in, into near-total isolation and impenetrability. I shared my feelings with no one.

Mercifully, the other part of school, the part that I had always loved, was still present: learning, reading, writing, and teachers. While my social and familial worlds were sometimes very difficult, this other world, one in which I thrived, was still available to me. I had teachers, those in English and History of course, who loved, favored, and nurtured me. Though I was a terrible music student who was always last-chair trombone, I loved music deeply and wanted very much to be good at it, to do justice at least to its beauty and power. It turned out later that I had a decent tenor voice and could carry a tune. I enjoyed student clubs and organizing and leading activities that brought about learning. I loved learning rudimentary French and Spanish and reading history books, Shakespeare, long novels, and poetry. (And secretly, and I've never told this to anyone, I longed to run track but could not because of lack of strength and asthma; this interests me now for what it means for that time: running: running for/from what?) In this respect, school was wonderful, until something nearly calamitous occurred: I read books that negated my existence.

In high school, I was wounded by two books and a teacher's reading of one of these books that I was required to read for classes. Of course, there were many other wounds, inflicted by students and teachers alike—name calling and/ or general pronouncements on groups of people—but in reading and learning, which I had loved so much, which was not an escape but a clarification, the pain was much harder to endure. The wall I had built was more permeable than I had imagined. First, as a junior in English class, while reading *The Great Gatsby*, a teacher whom I loved and whom I know loved me, made a point of condemning F. Scott Fitzgerald's anti-Semitism while praising his heterosexism and homophobia in this important, well-written, early twentieth-century U.S.

novel. She pointed out that Mr. McKee, "a pale feminine man from the flat below" (34) was obviously a homosexual whose inability to shave properly marks him as different from the others. She went on to laugh about how homosexuals always work hard on their appearance only to fail at it eventually. A message about compulsory heterosexuality if ever there is one. Of course, the text validates this when Gatsby says, "Taking out my handkerchief, I wiped from his cheek the remains of spot of dried lather that had worried me all afternoon" (41). I turned red, certainly, at the mere mention of this idea and was pained by her hateful mocking. I do not remember even recalling this character or these events during my initial reading, but upon discussion and later readings I was chagrined, at least, believing that she was talking directly to me. Absurd, I know; real, nonetheless. How could I, a boy just recently shaving his own face, trying hard after shaving to clean up before school, not be wounded by this? And, to this day, I still think of that character and that classroom conversation as I clean up from shaving. I wonder if these kinds of messages ever go away or clear themselves up, if pain ever dissolves, or if it can be transformed. (Ultimately, I think yes).

The next year, my senior year, I would encounter this again, not directly in class discussion but simply during my own reading. While reading Emily Bronte's *Wuthering Heights* and being repulsed by the ubiquitous violence but interested in the class-critique and ill-fated matches, I was taken aback by the narrator and his hateful description of Linton Heathcliff as the sickly and feminine son who is party to evil. After the interpretation of *The Great Gatsby*, how could I not, again, find the character I identified as gay—right or wrong—both to be me and not be me? How could I not be hurt again by reading and interpretation if every gay person in a book is somehow wrong or evil? My love for language and narrative, for the entire concept of reading, was challenged: if that which had been so interrogative and soothing turned back on me, as so much else had, the question became not how could I go on loving it but what can I do now?

So, I did what I had to do: I kept my mouth shut, and I went to college.

Of course, there had been no question that I would go to college after an above average high school academic career: the question was *how* and *where* I would go to college. My family had no money for college applications and certainly no money for tuition, room and board, and/or books; with five children living on a small salary in rural southwest Missouri, money was so scarce that paying for one kid's college was out of the question. Furthermore, none of us could understand why a college would even charge a fee to apply. My parents said, *Don't you have to pay when you get there? There are better, more important things to do with money.* I had just assumed, naively, that education was free. With these constraints, I applied to the one college without an application fee that I could find. Culver-Stockton College, in northeast Missouri on the western bank of the Mississippi River, happened to be a private liberal arts school where I might indulge myself in reading great books, *in being required to read great books*, and a place where I might have a chance to make the beginnings of a new life.

No, this will not become the typical narrative in which the son goes to college on both scholarships (and many loans, of course), attains education, lives a bourgeois life, and, as a consequence, sees his first homelife differently and then rejects it. I had already seen it differently: I knew that something, many things, were very wrong. I knew that a controlling and abusive father, a man frustrated by lack of money, privilege, and power because of his societal status was wrong. I knew that a controlled and beleaguered mother, someone trying to have some pleasure in life but unable to find it, was wrong. I knew that the direction in which my siblings were headed, the direction they have often followed—drug addiction, arrests, abuse, unemployment—was all wrong. (I am happy to write that some of my siblings are now clean and doing very well). I knew that the desire both to be somewhere else and with them was impossible to actualize and painful to comprehend. I knew that the small town in which we lived, a place that cannot be called a community, was wrong for its laughable classism and virulent racism, heterosexism, sexism, that believing poor people, people of color, gays and lesbians, the disabled, and women were less-than-human was wrong. I knew that the school system in which I had received most of my primary education was like most other institutions, merely a microcosm of the idiocy of the larger world, complete with its bigotry-in-power and its moribund ideas. But I did not possess, or even have access to, the language that would help me to understand, both emotionally and intellectually, what all this meant and what the future could be. (And at this time, when I was 17 and leaving for college, I had no doubt that a good future was available to me; now, with the world in the state it is in, in the state it has always been, I worry about a future for anything). It would be sometime, more than a year after finishing the BA, before I could read and apply to my own life these words from Toni Morrison's *Nobel Lecture in Literature*: "Oppressive language does more than represent violence; it is violence; it does more than represent the limits of knowledge; it limits knowledge. . . . Sexist language, racist language, theistic language, all are typical of the policing languages of mastery and cannot, do not permit new knowledge or encourage the mutual exchange of ideas" (14). Leaving home and going into higher education led me to find texts, like Morrison's, that allowed me to put words with ideas and feelings; going to college and graduate school enabled me to turn chaos and disorder into some kind of coherent meaning.

An example, perhaps my most salient one, comes from when I found and read, on my own, Audre Lorde's poetry. Reading her words, understanding her meanings, listening to her clear, strong voice on the page enabled me to put together the disparate thoughts swirling in my brain, those thoughts that kept me awake at night wondering what anything meant. There I was, a gay white guy from the working class, working on a Master's degree in English at Southwest Missouri State University (now Missouri State University), unable to use language—to talk with or to anyone—to free myself from the constraints placed on me by bigotry and misunderstanding and, finally, to begin talking with others. Lorde's poem, "Echoes," opened up language and the world to me:

There is a timbre of voice
that comes from not being heard
and knowing   you are not being
heard   noticed only
by others   not heard
for the same reason. (7)

Although Emily Dickinson says, "If I feel physically as if the top of my head were taken off, I know that is poetry," I must say that when my head is put back on, I know I've read poetry. Now, through Lorde's poem, I had a language in which to talk and to recontextualize everything about myself, everything I knew: that racism, ethnocentrism, classism, caste systems, sexism, gender hierarchy, heterosexism, ableism, ageism, regionalism, nationalism, speciesism, and environmental destruction were/are the problems coming from capitalism and patriarchy—and, importantly, that I both benefited from and lost myself in these machinations. I had been right: I was not wrong, and I had a voice that I could, must use to make things that are wrong right. I went on to find Lorde's essays in *Sister Outsider* and learned to understand and say that the "master's tools will never dismantle the master's house" and that

> [t]hose of us who stand outside the circle of this society's definition of acceptable women; those of us who have been forged in the crucibles of difference—those of us who are poor, who are lesbians, who are Black, who are older—know that survival is not an academic skill. It is learning how to stand alone, unpopular and sometimes reviled, and how to make common cause with those others identified as outside the structures in order to define and seek a world in which we can all flourish. (112)

Clearly, Lorde's language, coming from and foundational for the thoughts of Black Lesbian Feminism, helped me to see and hear everything anew; Lorde reached across time and space, through print and voice, and helped a young, chronically ill, gay white boy from the lower working class to become a radically feminist being doing the work that he needs to do, living a life that he needs to live. Her words help/ed me to read and reread; they help/ed me to live and relive.

It was and has been *learning in and outside* higher education, both undergraduate and graduate schools, that gave/ has given me the language to articulate a more complete, complex understanding of my personal and political relations to myself and to the rest of the world. This has been my liberation, my being set free from the multiple oppressions of classism, heterosexism, racism, sexism, ableism, ageism, and biospheric destruction. Going to college, but more specifically graduate school at Southwest Missouri State University and Northern Illinois University and reading black feminist poets, novelists, and essayists and understanding the radical potential in Shakespeare's outsider-bastards, Aaron,

Jacques, Edmond, has enabled me to confirm that I had not been wrong, that I am not wrong: that my being is more than okay; it's acceptable and necessary. I didn't exactly need a boost to my self-esteem; I simply needed some questions to be answered, some confirmation. Finding these literary and cultural texts and a few supportive, good friends has allowed me to answer my urgent, unformed questions and to find ways to tear down that wall of false invulnerability, to connect with others, and to begin to attempt to flourish as a being in the world.

I must admit, uncomfortably so, that I never questioned the idea that education belonged to me, that reading and learning were mine to be indulged and enjoyed, and that I would someday be a teacher or professor and do something good in the world. I was a good student in high school, and my teachers encouraged, helped, and indulged me. In higher education, I have/found professors to do the same. This has led me to believe that neither am I a *stranger in paradise* nor have I landed in *this fine place so far from home*,[1] for the academy is neither paradisiacal nor fine, even if it is a better space than other spaces. (I have to remind people all that time that better does not mean good: better simply means not as bad as something before or something else, which implies that the fully right is still to be achieved.) While (the) institutions of higher education are troubled and beset with multiple oppressions emanating from law makers' positions, taxpayers' desires, administrators' restraints, and some professors' and students' needs, the actual task, joy, and love of learning have been available to me; they should be available to everyone.

Of course, I am now able to understand more clearly, after years of reading and writing and collaborating with others, what it means that all this has been open to me; this means that white boys who meet some of the arbitrary standards can be given a pass, can have an entrance into the life of the mind or access to a decent paycheck. But, to be honest, the issue is more complicated. In order to survive throughout much of my life, I have had to be silent about social class, sexuality, race, ethnicity, gender, age, ability, and the environment—at times while in college and graduate school and certainly in my current job at a conservative community college on the edges of suburban and rural Illinois. I could not/have not been allowed to interrogate or protest openly what I saw/see to be wrong—the ridicule of lower class people; the open hostility and bigotry directed at sexual others; the obvious exclusion and stereotyping of people of color; the derogatory "jokes" made at women's expense; the refusal to acknowledge dis/abled people and people outside a particular age-range as fully human and valuable; the barefaced disregard for and abuse of other animals and ecosystems—without ramification. I could not acknowledge my own pain and/or privileges, and I have had plenty of both. With the language I learned on my own from the springboard of the academy and in collaboration with professors and other students, I can articulate a position that validates my claims that I am no stranger in a fine paradise and that I and all other beings and non-beings laboring and choking under oppressions of any kind must take what we can from education and use it to create a new, radically different world. I now understand that growing up as an/other in this culture was a benefit, not a liability. I understand more clearly that growing up poor and working class and being chronically ill, that being surrounded by people who are not deceitful or pretentious but genuinely helpful and caring, gives me the ability to be the same: to be myself, to be honest, and to love the earth and its inhabitants. And growing up gay, I think, enabled me to understand what compounded outsider status really is: that to be alone and ridiculed is painful and that to acknowledge pain is crucial for healing and living and, eventually, flourishing. I suppose being gay, disabled, and working class has allowed me to feel

85

sympathy and empathy not only for other people but for other creatures and things as well; this location, these pieces of my identity, has/have enabled me to connect, help, and flourish.

Writing this narrative, and reflecting back on painful and pleasurable episodes in my life, has been a most difficult task. Reliving so many memories and choosing and editing what to share (and what *not* to share) in order to attempt to make clear my meaning but not to violate myself or others could be at times overwhelming and disconcerting. No doubt, this narrative seems disorganized, or at least, disjunctive, perhaps foreshortened, even pointless. But isn't that the way memory and geography exist? Isn't this how we come to meaning, even if that meaning is unstable and temporary? Meanings are fragmented, patchy, often disconnected; our task as humans with consciousness, I think, is to attempt to connect, to build bridges to one another across time, space, politics, true or false consciousness, location, and locution, and then come together for what is good and right. I cannot say with honesty that I could understand or believe this if I had different origins or different educational experiences.

Just the other day, I finished reading Zadie Smith's novel, *On Beauty*. It is an excellent novel by a brilliant writer, but it is more than just good writing, more than novelistic virtuosity. Its meaning is profound, I think. Structured loosely on and going beyond E.M. Forster's novel *Howard's End*, Smith's *On Beauty* interrogates humans' relations with ourselves, others, and the worlds in which we live in a way that few novels can or do. The novel brings together people of seemingly dissimilar backgrounds, from different places, with different ideas, and forces them to communicate, perhaps even to resolve, their differences. In short, two of the characters, Kiki Belsey and Carlene Kipps, women of the African diaspora, wives of academic men on opposite sides of all issues, men who dominate all they participate in, including their marriages, come together and learn from each other that to hear one another, to be open and vulnerable, that to share and to love, is to flourish. I will not give away the novel's ending or meaning, but I will tell you this: at the last moment, when virtually all is lost, the reader finds out that one of the women has written the other a note with the words that tear down the unnecessary walls we build, the words that help us into being a radically new world: *"There is such a shelter in each other."*

Works Cited

Bronte, Emily. *Wuthering Heights*. 1848. New York: Penguin, 1996.

Fitzgerald, F. Scott. *The Great Gatsby*. 1925. New York: Simon & Schuster, 1995. 34.

Forster, E.M. *Howards End*. 1910. New York: Penguin, 2000.

Lorde, Audre. "Echoes." *The Marvelous Arithmetics of Distance*. New York: Norton, 1993. 7.

————. "The Master's Tools Will Never Dismantle the Master's House." *Sister Outsider: Essays and Speeches by Audre Lorde*. Freedom, CA: Crossing, 1984. 112.

Morrison, Toni. *The Nobel Lecture in Literature, 1993*. New York: Knopf, 1996. 16.

Smith, Zadie. *On Beauty*. New York: Penguin, 2005. 431.

Wharton, Edith. *A Backward Glance*. 1934. New York: Simon & Schuster, 1998. xix.

Note

[1] Titles from two early texts about academics from the working class: *Strangers in Paradise: Academics from the Working Class*, ed. Jack Ryan and Charles Sackrey (Boston: South End, 1984) and *This Fine Place so far from Home: Voices from Academics from the Working Class,* ed. C.L. Barney Dews and Carolyn Leste Law (Philadelphia: Temple UP, 1995).

II. Direct from Moon City

MARCUS CAFAGÑA

Nicely Woven Inside

I have a photograph of my late wife
holding up a necktie for the camera.
It's actually the back of the tie she displays—
its inner lining. *Nicely woven inside*
were the words the Italian vendor used
to describe it. I took the shot of her
on a street corner in Rome shortly after
she noticed the triangular flaps of fabric
not stitched together when the casing of the tie
came undone. With manicured fingernails
she pinched the silken folds of the tie open
to reveal what I'd missed—the hand painting
on the inner lining of a woman in the nude.
I caught Dianne right before she burst
into a real fit of laughter, the kind
that seldom possessed her, which came
first in snorts, then tears. And though the joke
was on me, I had to laugh too, laugh
at what the vendor, in his poor English,
must really have said: *naked woman inside*.
I can't be sure, but I think he winked,
and I don't know what became of the trick tie
or the woman inside.

Marcus Cafagña

The Death Sale

About the time the shock deadens to sorrow,
deadens to leaves crackling underfoot,
our daughter holds a sale in the yard
with little stickers on anything that was Dianne's:
a hundred belts, counting the plastic one
she had practiced hanging herself with,
enough blush to paint a thousand masks,
a table full of vitamins, another strewn
with books by her idol, Tennessee Williams,
his restlessness, his sleeplessness like hers,
their streetcar named desire going nowhere.
It's my idea to sell the furniture, washer, drier,
waveless waterbed, as if now that she's gone,
I'll never need to wash or sleep again.
My neighbors don't mind robbing the grave.
One teenage girl opens a compact,
thinks she looks beautiful in too much make-up,
smears on the garish rouge that came with
Dianne's French maid get-up. Everything sells
except her menagerie of stiletto heels.
Just before evening, a woman in white scrubs
models the platforms from France, sighing
Oh, Paris! She's skeletal thin, like Dianne,
loves her legs in kinky boots from Milan,
cradles a pair of pumpkin-colored pumps.
In Philipino English, she tells me these are shoes
no barrio nurse back home could afford.

It hurts to know the shoes are just her size—
that they mean to her what they meant to Dianne.
But I won't take her money, say if my wife
were alive, she'd want her to have them,
these shoes Dianne hoped would help her walk
out of one life and into the fantasy of another.

Marcus Cafagña

Possessive

It seems like just the other day
although it's been years
since Dianne was alive.

If she were, she'd pin me
to a chair, straddle a leg
on either side of mine.

After all this time
she'd still search my face
for white heads or black.

Even when we were dating,
she considered it a duty
to rush the ferocity

of her love toward me
with no warning
but the rustle of a skirt.

JANE HOOGESTRAAT

Winter Stitching

An old embroidery pattern, strands
of magenta, spring green, pastime
during a long winter, folded away
for years in a cedar chest somewhere,

lost by now, except in memory
like the light caught by indoor flowers
whose names I tend now, *bromeliad*,
coleus, strange unpoetic terms, odd

seasons, as if beauty should speak,
or will again in the quieter rooms,
of the simple care one takes with a life,
however unseen or among others.

But there is always more to learn,
varieties of *coleus, dappled apple,*
kiwi fern, color evident enough,
also, *dark star, dark heart*

how to explain beauty there
as it winds on fragile green stems
toward spring light, also *caladium*
grown from seeds turned to thin bulbs

sprouting out of almost nowhere,
among what my friend calls
the *wandering jewel*, thereby sparing
me having to learn the Latin phrase.

And the newest addition, *Persian shield*,
imported from some obscure tropic,
rare, precious in its own right this year
of new names for almost everything.

JANE HOOGESTRAAT

Off the Interstate
from *Harvesting All Night*

She was drinking tea, not dressed for weather,
smoking, counting loose change to collect
enough for a meal? And writing. In mid-winter
at a truck stop, the rigs with their thunder
but far from any town. How to measure
that memory, ask for a late blessing?

I will never know her story, she the blessing,
the haunting way her face pale with weather
reminds me of others' isolation. That measure
balancing small complaints, as in the collect
to make no peace with oppression, the thunder
silenced in sub-zero glare, years ago, in winter.

To be that alone in light clothes in winter
frightens me, solitude with no blessing,
the endless interstate, the blizzard, no thunder
to prepare the heart for calmer weather.
The gesture of how words and change collect,
provide the hours with their own measure.

I trust those earliest of memories, measure
of a child paying attention, in a long winter
over a half-eaten plate, sorting images to collect
the stories, traveling that land. With a blessing
if not of peace then of clarity, weather
of compassion. What remains after the thunder.

In summer, heat lightning without thunder
cracks open miles of landscape, to measure
the harsh, extreme swings of climate, weather
that marks this country desolate. Less so in winter
when austerity might emerge as a blessing,
a sky acute in its pink cold, an image to collect.

Whether she rode away, went home to collect
more clothes or left later, after the thunder,
set off older, secure in her search for a blessing,
a kinder version of herself, a way to measure
the distance between the drifter she was that winter
and the surer self emerging from such weather. . . .

How do we measure distance, remember the collect
in mid-winter, *to contend against evil*, thunder,
and odd weather, before the impossible blessing?

CERAMICS BY PAIGE FREESEMAN

Ceramic 1

Etched Ceramic 2

BILLY CLEM

Bachelor Buttons

> It takes years to learn how to look at the destruction
> Of beautiful things;
>
> To learn how to leave the place
> Of oppression;
>
> And how to make your own regeneration
> Out of nothing.
>
> —Gerald Stern
> "When I Have Reached the Point of Suffocation"

For my twentieth birthday, you sent
a present of bachelor buttons.

I planted the seeds in father's flower bed
where they came up purple and pink but died

next to those Van Gogh-yellow dandelions
we failed to weed out.

Years later, a young baritone sings
Erklönig on the radio, and I wonder if those flowers

were a gift. Confirmation, perhaps. Or a nod toward
acknowledgement, something father cannot bestow

even now. He hated the buttons and said so,
for he could not know, as you knew, that behind

every kiss lies
pain, that nothing forced together stays.

100

BILLY CLEM

Today in the Missouri Ozarks

For Steven Skaggs and Ruth Austin

> Mais voici qu'à mon tour
> J'abandonne les petites villes de mon enfance
> Je te les offer
> Dans la plénitude
> De leur solitude
>
> Comprends-tu bien le présent redoubtable?
> Je te donne d'étranges petites villes tristes,
> Pour le songe.*
>
> —Anne Hébert
> "Les Petites Villes"

Today in the Missouri Ozarks it is
75°. Though early January, young
girls in cropped t-shirts and Capri pants
prepare to tan as they group in their fathers' cul-de-sacs
and flirt with the season's premature advances.
Their white skins absorb and buffet
a southerly wind that blows vaguely unwanted.

And we wonder, later, 6 or so in early evening,
why a three-quarters moon,
like a yo-yo returning to the cupped, upside down hand,
crawls up a sky bottom-edged by
thin evergreens and sweet gums still leaving.

These girls, just fourteen years old now, maybe,
will marry too soon the sons of those Scots-Irish
and Easterners who came here centuries ago,

sons of men who cleared mountain forests and their peoples,
whose women stood dumb and unready for what was to come.

* But now it's my turn.
  I abandon the small towns of my youth.
  I offer them to you
  In the fullness
  Of their loneliness.

  Do you really understand this dreadful gift?
  I give you strange small towns
  For dreams.

—Anne Hébert
"Small Towns"

BILLY CLEM

neither elegy nor sonnet

In Memoriam, Jan Arwood

the philodendron
you gave me long ago
wilts from its pot,
its once-green vines weak,

its leaves browning
from the windowsill
it nearly touches the couch
where you sat

after weeks of radiation
your long curly
hair thin and falling out

your skin splashed with a
brown like the dirt in that pot:
dry, hard, impervious to water or light

BEN PFEIFFER

The Lexicon of the Sword

He would not have lived more comfortably, as acquaintances and distant relatives assured him, in some outlying time and culture—the 16th century, say. People thought so, knowing him only as the *maestro* of his antiquated school, consultant to film stars, a self-styled swashbuckler. They remembered how his mentor, Fredrik Rosenthal, had been before he died, always claiming to miss France, always photographed with a saber in his hand or sheathed prominently at his side.

In truth, Nikolai Kolovin enjoyed the mechanical comforts of his adopted America: the click of laptop computer keys, the iPod on the waistband of his gym shorts, the bumblebee buzz of his microwave when it heated his wife's leftover meatloaf. He did not long for the rigging of a Napoleonic schooner. He never lost his head in daydreams of cobblestone streets. The chiaroscuro film sets on which he consulted—laden with artificial fog and alternating pools of light and darkness—embodied magic only in two dimensions of celluloid. Whenever someone said to him, Nik, you just don't belong here with us, he said to them, Is that so, and lifted his drink to hide a smile.

Never mind, Anna would say. Let them think what they want.

"What's it like to work with Martin Scorsese?" his wife's friend asked him.

He thought her name might be Allison Neubright, but he couldn't be sure. Anna counted a significant percentage of the metropolitan population as friends, and sometimes

Nikolai had trouble keeping them all straight. So many friends—as opposed to acquaintances—was an unusual state of mind. In fifty-three years, for himself, he counted two great friends. One was Anna, of course, and the other was a betrayer, dead to him, and would forever remain so.

Questions made him uncomfortable, especially at parties like this. She pressed him. "Come on, speak up so we can hear you."

A small crowd—drawn together by the crooning note in Allison's voice—watched him expectantly. Allison set her drink on the head of the grand piano and crossed her arms, an upside down exclamation point in a satin, ebony halter. He stood with his back to the bay window in the living room. Henry Robin's bungalow—modeled as a Tuscan villa, resplendent in white, beige, polished walnut, and iron accents—overlooked the lights of Los Angeles, making a microchip from the streetlamps, traffic signals, and emergency blinkers on the city's endless highway.

Now, with his back to this toy city, Nikolai Kolovin was trapped, cornered, unable even to leap to his death. He began to sweat and swirl the ice in his bourbon glass. He could feel the onlookers examining his left eye, his one good eye, which amplified his self-consciousness. He hated to address more than one person at a time because of his limited field of vision and because of his broken English. Anna told him he spoke better than most natives, an encouraging lie, but her love didn't change his Cyrillic tint on the pronunciations. Or his mangling of even the most cliché expressions.

"Martin Scorsese?" he asked.

"Yes," Allison said. "You worked with him, right? Some kind of sword fighting movie?"

"Fencing," Nikolai said. "Yes, Scorsese. He is a very smart man. I didn't see him much while we shot the film . . . I work with actors and stuntmakers mostly."

When he finished he felt as if he had delivered the commencement address at a university. The crowd around the piano—polite women with bobbed hair and painted lips; flabby, tan men straining to look cleverer than they really were—nodded as if they accepted his answer.

Nikolai looked around for Anna. Where had she wandered off to? He needed an excuse to leave before the conversation turned.

"How did you lose your eye?" a man asked, and his wife slapped his chest lightly.

"Honey!" she said. "Don't be rude."

"It is all right," Nikolai said to her. "I was in fencing competition in Berlin. I was fencing against my *maestro*, Herr Rosenthal, and with the tip of his épée—a practice sword, a foil—he stuck me in the eye. We were practicing without our gear, which is beginner's mistake."

"How old were you?"

"I was thirty-four," Nikolai said, "and he was ninety-two."

"Did you get compensation?" another man asked. "Reparations or anything?"

"Obviously you didn't know Fredrik Rosenthal," Nikolai said.

Allison's husband, James Neubright, stepped up behind his wife and snaked a wide-fingered hand around her waist. Nikolai couldn't remember the man's occupation. Neubright's weak chin trembled slightly. Even in the twilight, Nikolai could tell Neubright had filled his belly with half a dozen Whiskey Sours. His voice slurred beneath the gentle Italian concerto piping through the bungalow's stereo system. Jim Neubright held his latest drink up so his wife could lean forward and take a sip. She steadied his glass with a bejeweled hand.

"Your *maestro* sounds like a cocksucker," Jim Neubright said.

106

"So maybe you did know him," Nikolai said, and everyone laughed.

"I heard about your school," Neubright said. His voice stayed perfectly flat. "Shame, that. Such a fucking *shame.*"

Nikolai blinked and lifted his drink to take a sip. To buy himself time to think. Neubright walked a few paces to the edge of the carpet. He took a hold of the cuff on Nikolai's jacket and Nikolai allowed himself to be turned away. He could feel the crowd behind them, a silent chorus, tense and waiting, judging their tiniest movements and inflections. James Neubright leaned in drunkenly and dropped his voice several octaves. The purpose of the drop was theatre, not privacy.

"I heard about what Thom Roberts did at your fencing school," Neubright said. "We all heard. It was on CNN, Kolovin."

Nikolai held very still, feeling stupid and threatened. He saw the elliptical droplets at Neubright's temples, smelled the dark liquor on his breath, and resisted the urge to tighten his fingers around Neubright's fleshy jowls.

"You should have known better," Neubright said.

"I didn't know about any of it, Jim," Nikolai said. Unconsciously his knees bent. His calloused hands massaged one another, and, without remarking on it, he popped his knuckles. The air bubbles in his joints sounded very loud to his ears. "Anna and I have a little boy, too. He is called Sasha."

"Sasha?" Neubright said with feigned nostalgia. "Sounds like the name of a faggot I knew up at UC Berkeley."

"It is a Russian nickname for Alexander," Nikolai said. Then, furious for explaining himself, for explaining his *son,* he felt his control slipping away. The thought of violence against this man suddenly became a very concrete possibility in his mind. His temper tightened a fist and readied a blow that would send Jim Neubright crashing through the glass and tumbling off the mountain into the blackness at the edge of the California universe.

"That's enough, Jim," Anna said. Though she stood at least seven inches shorter than either of them, she stepped between both men and hooked her arm through Nikolai's at the elbow. Her eyes were hurt and fiery. With her free hand she brushed a curl of dark hair out of her eye: a self-conscious, defensive gesture Nikolai had always loved, because he thought it gave the impression that she could see more clearly than anyone else.

"You should be ashamed of yourself," she said. "Jesus, Jim."

Jim Neubright shook himself, collected his thoughts. He fussed with the crease of his pinstripe jacket. His class ring, the gold effigy of a snarling bear, glinted in the diffused light. "You're right, Anna," he said. "I'm sorry, Nik. I just get too worked up when I drink. I hope you know it's just the Jack Daniel's talking. It's just . . . I heard a rumor . . . " He paused and looked over his shoulder to make sure his audience was still listening. "I heard you posted his bail. Is that true?"

"I posted bail," Nikolai said. He felt the white-hot rage seep out of his muscles and dissipate. He looked at Anna, then, but she gave no indication of her thoughts. "To tell you the truth, Thom Roberts, he is no friend of mine."

At home Nikolai excused himself to his study. The babysitter was watching a late-night program on television when they arrived. Sasha had fallen asleep under his Spider-man comforter with Tony the Pony, his stuffed giraffe, squeezed under his arm. The babysitter was a graduate student with a matronly smile. A sweet girl, and good humored. Nikolai wrote her check with a mixture of shameful gratitude and relief. Anna hung their jackets without a word, kissed Sasha goodnight, and went into the bedroom to remove her makeup and her earrings. Nikolai loved how she never pressured him to talk. She knew when he was ready he would come to her.

"I'm going back out, Anya," he told her when the babysitter had left.

"Be careful," she said. "I love you."

"I love you, too," he said. "*Ya tebya lublu, toja.*"

She kissed him goodnight and went into their bedroom. He walked down the hall to look in on his son. The boy was curled up with his knees to his chest and his eyes shut tight. Nikolai kissed him on the forehead and shut his door quietly, leaving a crack for light from the hallway.

He went to his study and locked the door behind him. He sat in his reading chair for fifteen minutes, listening to the noises of his home, the creak of carpet tacked to hardwood, the whisper of dust-furred fan blades turning overhead.

After a while, the *maestro* took down his sword from the wall-mounts above his writing desk. Ancient, tempered steel, cool to the touch. The cornerstone of the Kolovin family collection. He held it away from him and tested its weight. This sword was unlike the practice foil, the épée, or the saber he used when he taught classes at the Academy. It was a dueling sword, a rapier, the choice weapon for intimate combat in the 17th century. He ran the pads of his fingers over the gold on the hilt, handguard, and pommel. A fine sword—European style, Russian craft. The blade had belonged to his ancestor, a Russian brigadier general under Pyotr Alexeyevich Romanov—Peter the Great—and legend suggested that Ibrahim Hannibal, the great-grandfather of Alexander Pushkin and Peter's godson, had gifted the sword to the *maestro*'s ancestor. Nikolai Kolovin didn't know if the story was true or if it mattered. Usually he enjoyed the idea that the African general might have gifted the sword to his family in friendship, but tonight, as he held the sword balanced in front of him, the thought offered little comfort.

He placed his foot forward and lowered into the traditional *en guard* stance for épée combat. He ignored the coffee tables and couches, and he stood perfectly balanced, rapier stretched out in his left arm, an extension of his body. Across the room his eye lingered on pictures of Sasha at his fourth birthday party. The boy had his mother's Native American eyes. The ink-black irises of Iroquois blood.

The *maestro* raised his right arm up for balance. He kept his sword hand—his left hand—in a partially supinated position.

In traditional épée fencing, competitors fought bouts to one touch. He could hear Fredrik Rosenthal's voice say the words. It made historical sense, because épée bouts reflected the abrupt, violent nature of rapier duels. One hole punched in an opponent and the game was over. Today, for more sport, duels were carried on to five touches. Double-touches still counted as one point for each athlete. If you strike each other at once, two holes are made, one in each épéeist. Both players, in a sense, have gained nothing. Both players lose a touch.

He stripped off his party clothes and dressed himself in his gear. He fastened each piece deliberately. Fingers flexed in the white mesh glove with the blood-red stripe (only one glove, the left one). He worked quietly so he wouldn't wake Sasha and Anna. When he was finished he slipped the rapier into a scabbard. He took his overcoat and a second rapier from the closet by the door. Then he picked up a first edition of the book from his grandfather's bookcase.

The bestselling phenomena, white letters on navy paper—*The Lexicon of the Sword*. He loved the rhetoric of it, the intellectualism of "lexicon," the traditional brutality and elegance of "sword." He flipped to the rear dustjacket flap. Two strangers smiled out at him from the 3 x 4 black-and-white glossy above their names: Thomas M. Roberts & Nikolai Kolovin. Best friends. Brothers. Thomas stood with his swordpoint resting in the grass at his feet, arms crossed in a posture so casual it could only be fake. Yes, fake. That was the word. He dazzling smile still shone from under the gloss that preserved it. Nikolai was smiling too, black hair and white skin, while he held Ibrahim Hannibal's blade pointed straight out of the picture and into the camera lens. It was a dynamic photograph.

Nikolai Kolovin sniffed, closed the book, and returned it to the shelf.

A janitor found Thomas Roberts and a student together in a practice room on August 8th, 2008. The janitor's name was Jerri Seer, and that night she had waxed the gym floors, vacuumed the offices, emptied the wastebaskets, and smoked a cigarette before punching out. In the hallway near the break room, Jerri had noticed a light on in one of the fencing courts. She made a mental note to turn it off on her way out. The older woman had been employed at the Academy for five years, since its inception, and remained loyal to her boss, Mr. Kolovin. She didn't describe exactly what she saw Thom Roberts doing with the boy to the media. She would tell the jury, she said, and if the judge decided to allow cameras at the hearing then they could find out like everybody else. She wouldn't be the ringmaster at this goddamn circus, she told them. Then she lit a cigarette and blew smoke into their microphones. Until the proceedings her police report would remain confidential. It didn't matter, but Nikolai was grateful for the gesture.

In the meantime, the Academy was ruined. Everything Nikolai and Thom had worked so hard to build—brought down overnight. Parents withdrew their students from classes without explanation or notice. Nikolai Kolovin had been judged: Guilty by association. At night he drank vodka and imagined the emotional scars his friend had inflicted on the boy. How many others were there? He cursed himself for

111

not noticing sooner. He read and re-read the books he and Thom had written, marking out Thom's passages with a fat black marker. He left the dissected texts stacked around his office, including a manuscript of the sequel to *The Lexicon of the Sword*, titled *The Encyclopedia of Dueling*, which would have taught advanced techniques to fans of the first book. Before his publisher called and canceled the deal, that was, and before his agent stopped taking his calls.

More students came forward, parents' hands on the small of their backs, and admitted that they, too, had been molested by Roberts the Fencing Master. How many children could I have saved if I had been more mindful? Nikolai wondered. And what of Sasha Kolovin? The boy appeared unharmed and had never been alone with Thom Roberts for more than a few minutes. He showed no signs of night terrors, eating disorders, or Severe Emotional Disturbance. He had never suffered physical abuse as the other children had, bruises on his forearms, broken fingers, or blows to the head, easily confused with the usual practice injuries. But the thought that it could have happened—that it could have happened to his son, his beautiful Sasha—nauseated Nikolai and brought spasms to his muscles and pain so white and cold he had only felt it once before, when he had lost a piece of himself in Berlin.

When Nikolai lost his right eye at the International Traditional Fencing Competition in Berlin, Germany, Thom reminded him of what Herr Rosenthal, their beloved *maestro*, told them when they studied together under him at his famous school in Oslo, Norway: "You may always tell a fencing master from a hobbyist, because he will always have only one eye." Thom pronounced the sentence with Rosenthal's German lilt. He balanced on the edge of the hospital bed and touched the back of Nikolai's hand, where the IV needle broke the skin.

"I am sorry about your eye, boy," Fredrik Rosenthal told him later.

"No, you're not," Nikolai said.

"There are worse things to lose," Rosenthal said. "But I am sorry."

Ninety-two year old Fredrick Rosenthal taught and fenced from sheer willpower, since by the time they came to learn from him he was an unsteady old man, twitchy and given to bursts of temper. He would throw chairs in the lofts where he held classes, strike students with the flat of his hand, or break décor and windows with his fists. Most of the vases and breakable things had been removed (or destroyed) by the school's fifteenth year, when Thom and Nikolai enrolled, unaware of how their lives would someday become connected.

The first day they stood together, waiting for their lesson, Rosenthal hurled a rotary telephone at a student who could not produce an acceptable triple-inverse cuff rotation. The phone sailed over the student's head and smashed a window overlooking the alley behind his studio. Nik and Thom's first classes were held in the freezing air of Norway's late September, with only a space heater—produced, as if by magic, from a forgotten attic or storeroom—to warm their frozen appendages. Rosenthal seemed like a demon to Nikolai, because the cold did not touch him. He smoked gold-filtered cigarettes continuously and dropped the ashes and butts anywhere he felt was reasonable. He offered no apology for his fit of temper after, and no warning before his next outburst. The student who escaped bludgeoning by telephone quit that day and never returned. Nikolai did not blame him.

Perhaps, he thought, lying in the West Berlin hospital, I should have joined him.

After the student fled that day, Rosenthal turned to them, the Russian and the American, and hooked his meaty thumbs behind his belt. He puffed out his sunken chest.

"I make no apologies ever," he said. "The fencing sport was born of swordplay. Very violent. The history of fencing is the history of wars. Empires from Japan to England rose and fell on the backs of their swordsmen. Romans, too. Even after bow and arrows come, these terrible weapons that pierce armor, swords remain. Later, after pistols and gunpowder come, swords are for settling personal disputes between friends and rivals. So do you want to learn to fight like men or will you run like this boy?"

"No, sir," Nikolai said.

"And you—American?"

"No, sir," Thom said.

"Good. To train a young gentleman in the art of the sword, since someday he might need to fight, techniques were developed that allowed blades to be crossed without spilt blood. These techniques were developed for centuries and packaged as different styles. This is traditional fencing. The Italian style, for example, places emphasis on kinetic motion and brute force. My own French style, by contrast, stresses the importance of footwork, form, and subtlety. Each style possesses its own merits and faults. To be a master, a *maestro*, one must know all styles intimately. Do you understand what I am telling you?"

"Yes, sir."

"Yes, sir."

"Then pick up your foils," Rosenthal said, "and let us begin."

Within hours the streaming video appeared on the Internet. In the grainy film, two men can be seen talking together in the darkness outside the Saddle Ranch restaurant on Sunset Boulevard. The open-air deck remains deserted except for a

114

nervous waitress. Framed by limestone fence, the two figures continued to argue, oblivious to the student film crew with their Canon XLS digital camera. The Argyle Hotel shadowed them in the background, an obelisk of Old Hollywood. CNN fact-finders positively identified the two arguing men forty-five minutes later as former business partners Thomas Michael Roberts and Nikolai Efimovich Kolovin, a Russian expatriate.

Thom Roberts wore a cheap suit and his blue eyes were puffy and swollen. His hair and beard were untrimmed and twisted in curls of grease. He didn't look at Nikolai when they spoke. In the fluorescent light Thom seemed emaciated, a man built from steel bars, genuinely shrunken and sullen.

Nikolai knew long ago about Roberts's personality problems—they had been friends for over thirty years—such as to cry when no one paid attention to him, to cling to friends and women, to sink into a black rage if he didn't get what he wanted.

And yet the man was so intelligent, too, a genius of fencing technique and style, passionate about music and art. For years Nikolai had admired him.

"You can't beat me, Nik," Thom said. The skinny man fingered the hilt of the sword Nikolai had brought him. "I don't want to fight you. Why are you doing this?"

"I will explain you," Nikolai said. He had never felt self-conscious speaking in front of Thom. Now his voice shook. "All my life people say to me, 'You should have lived long ago, Nikolai. You are from another time.' This is not true. I like movie popcorn and indoor plumbing. Yet we live by an older code, too, do we not? Somehow we do this. Our *maestro* taught us this when he taught us the sword. What would Rosenthal say, Thom?"

"I don't know."

"He would say that I should kill you," Nikolai said. " 'It is your duty,' he would say."

"He wouldn't want you to kill me."

"*Da*, he would want you dead."

"You couldn't."

"I can and I will," Nikolai said.

"I'm sorry about everything."

"It doesn't matter."

"Doesn't it?"

"*Nyet.*"

"In that case," Thom said. He stood up from his chair, wiped the corners of his mouth with the napkin, and set it gently over his plate of cold food.

Before swords flashed, Nikolai punched Thom with his free hand. Not a movie punch but a real punch, all knuckles and force. Nikolai channeled all his hatred and anger and shock into the first blow. His friend made no movement to stop him; Thom took one dizzy step back and placed his right hand against the fence for support. Nikolai could just see the imprint of his Iroquois ring—the only piece of jewelry Anna ever bought him besides his wedding band— on Thom's cheek in the semidarkness, a tiny speck of blood just beneath his mouth where the stone had cut his face.

In the background someone yelled in surprise. The cameraman moved forward to frame a more cinematic angle. He said, "Are those real swords?"

Another voice said, "Is this a scene or something?"

Thom's feet went out from under him and he lowered his body to the sidewalk, using the wooden slats as a brace. The sword in his right hand clattered on the concrete. His teeth were coated in blood. His effeminate voice, sulky and dignified, was clogged because of his ruined nose. Nikolai held the tip of his blade to Thom's Adam's-apple, which bobbed up and down, skin scraping along the tapered point.

Thom leapt up, rolled sideways, snatched up his blade, and struck at Nikolai's exposed thigh. Nikolai danced backwards, parrying deftly, just quick enough to avoid Thom's blade biting his femoral artery. The waitress jumped clear, spilling a steaming dish of potatoes, roast beef, and cheese. Thom was on his feet again, slashing, yelling curses. The two men fenced around the tables and knotted-pine chairs.

Each man hopped the fence to the parking lot, eyes never flicking away, and continued to circle each other. The two valets—young, college-aged men—backed away nearer to the film crew and gave the fencers a wide berth.

Sparks; ringing steel; arcs of light.

Thom forced Nikolai back towards the traffic of Sunset Boulevard in a chess match of footwork. Nikolai stumbled as his boot slipped on the curb; Thom leapt up slightly and brought his blade around to strike at Nikolai's neck. Nikolai easily knocked the reckless attack away and brought his own sword up. He drove it up through Thom's shoulder beneath the joint.

On the video a disembodied voice, the voice of the amateur videographer, yelled out: "Jesus *Christ!* He stabbed him. Did you see that? He fucking killed that guy."

When Nikolai Kolovin wrenched his sword from Thom's shoulder the younger man fell to his knees with a cry. The blade made a sucking noise as it left his flesh. Thom knelt and pressed his hands to the wound, staunching the bleed, willing the blood to stay inside his body. Nikolai ran a gloved finger along the black edge of Ibrahim Hannibal's rapier. Thom's blood spread through the white in a bright stain. One hole punched in an opponent and the game was over, Nikolai Kolovin thought. If you strike at once, both players lose a touch.

In the distance, sirens sang mournfully, although most of the traffic failed to heed them, to stop or even slow down. A Cadillac Escalade swerved to avoid hitting the two men standing on the side of the road and the driver honked deafeningly as he blew past them.

Jewelry by Sam Hitchcock

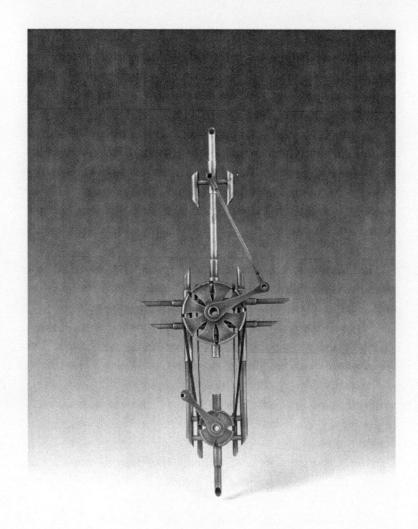

Piston

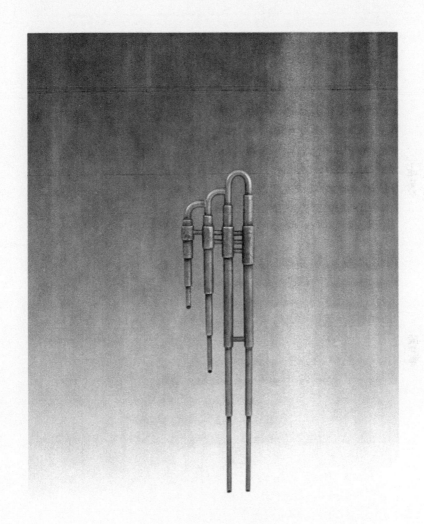

Untitled

LEE BUSBY

Key West, the Morning After Fantasy Fest

I sit alone at *Croissants de France*,
too early for the bars to open
but people are out, waiting,
walking in the sun.
There are no Vikings
or Angels in the street anymore,
no Hemingways or Frosts either.

I've been here all morning
and the orange juice on my table
is warm and the bacon has fallen
off of my Americanos croissant.

Two older men sit across the aisle
from me holding hands on the left side
of the table, forks on the right, with chest hair
coming out of their tank-tops like fingertips
reaching for their lipstick-smeared chins.

I've been here too long on a Sunday,
the breeze isn't cool, the street not so quiet.
I can see, coming down the sidewalk
with his family, a little boy
dressed like a barmaid, hopping
from shade tree to shade tree, his blonde hair
trailing him like an afterthought.
I bet to him I don't look like anybody.

Lee Busby

I Watch Jim

put on his coat and John Deere hat, grab
some coffee, go down the hill
next to his house. Out the window, I see
him open the wood-gate, balancing
the drink between arm and breast.

Walking on, he holds the mug close
to his lips, the other hand stretched
downward, palm open, brushing
the tops of the wheat. Annie, his palomino,
comes trotting up, and Jim reaches into his
pocket and pulls out something I can't see,
runs his hand under her mouth
and she takes it before running off.

He told me earlier that he misses his wife.
She's been gone five days now. She used
to walk through the field in the mornings,
first thing before breakfast, and she never
did like coffee. She insisted on buying
Annie, but never rode her in the four years
they've had her. He didn't know his wife
had a bad heart, and he couldn't drive
that Ford fast enough to the hospital.

I see him make his way over to the pond
and toss rocks into the water, waiting
for the waves to stop before he throws in another.
Annie circles behind and comes to the edge.
He doesn't pay her any mind.

LEE BUSBY

Grandma Says

One day he unplugged most everything
in the house because he couldn't get the TV
to come on. And just yesterday he said he left
a quart of prune juice on the tailgate
of some man's wagon and now
he ain't never going to get it back.

I've heard him go into his bedroom
and pray for the Lord to whop him
in the head because he's tired of living.
Once he even said he wouldn't care
if the devil did it, he just wants to be done.
He's the oldest of eight kids and has
outlived them all. He hates that.

I'm afraid to leave him home by himself
now, so I drag him to Wal-Mart
and flea-markets, even though he would
rather sit on the front porch swing all day
and keep hold of that old cat of his.

It's been a good thing since we started
sleeping in different rooms, that man kicks
in his sleep. I can only take that for fifty-three
years exactly, not any more than that.
But he keeps his light on late, here lately,
and I yell "Shut it off!" and he does.

But he fidgets, fidgets, I can hear him
moving around in the dark. I yell
"Cut it out!" and he does. And he makes
the coffee sometimes now because I don't
get up just because he gets up.
He sits close to me at the kitchen table.

LEE BUSBY

Bank Fishing

My father lies down,
nestles the rod in the crook
of his elbow, pulls on his hat
and waits, somber and quiet,
while I sit anxious to work
against the fish, eyes glued
to my bobber. I know if he falls
asleep, the slightest tug will move
his hand up off his chest
to ever-so-lightly grasp the pole
and give it a little pull,
running a finger over the line
that's as gray as his hair.

I imagine that line in the water
keeps him anchored to this bank
somehow and if it was cut,
broken from the pond,
he would begin to float up,
not knowing until I reached out,
caught the dangling line
and gave it a little tug,
that he had slipped,
almost, away from me.

Jennifer Smith

Translations from the French of Marie Melisou

What was Whispered in Fog's Ear

Life is a delicate love
like a sigh of boredom
a series of footpaths
in the form of parachute jumps
a long list of scars
and that of all the words consigned to darkness.

On certain days he said
for a long time we dared to live.

The sun is a shabby neon tube
in a sea green bar
an improbable hide and seek
where everything is still stowed away,
and the pencil lead
a kind of keystone in a ball of dark wool
spits my swarming disgust.

On certain evenings he said
I knew how to keep you warm.

Some seasonal words
pile upon themselves, haunt, hold at bay
combinations of frozen fragments
that play at leap frog.

The spirit of these places describes a feeling
a lack of existence
where daggers swim unbroken
and clairvoyants bleed smiles
swinging from here to there.

On certain nights he said
in fog's ear
I see you as if you were still there.

Sealed Indifference

On a limb made of ribbon
of my fog shrouded wasteland
where each idea stretches
from a nothing so immense,
exists an inane smile
little rest for the living
in troubled waiting
then dejected by colored seals.

A jar of wide open eyes
for looking again, observing how
I swallow a lingering sweetness
slow almost stopped
living in such little jumps

in the chemical hope
that day clouded vision exists.
I find in it a prominent possibility
glassy kneading an unstuck moment
a savage remainder forgetter of evil being.

Moment of urgency
for an outward bound mind
for an indifferent body
like falling wind

even the pain of wasting away forgets itself.

ARTHUR HUBER

The Apples, Darling

You should have seen the apples
from Mr. Filmore's farm:
strawberry rose beauties worth
biting, gently as you know.

The trees where I picked them
were marvelous, too: each gnarled
yet graceful, adults not hateful.
I brought them home in the basket

You thatched from husks, but
darling, I couldn't find you.
And the apples, darling, those
Apples turned the color of rust.

NATHAN MASTERS

The Burning of Paper, The Melting of Wax

That grove of birch pulling through the dirt's ridged gums
that we might have become, the curls and creases
of its bark which littered the low foliage like discarded pages,
where we walked, where you gave to each trunk the name
of a poet as if the roots drew ink, their boughs:
a strict calligraphy above caught-wind grass that could,
if we read it, take us along the unfollowed paths
of owls, or as if their leaves, rustling at night against our
windows, wrote arrhythmic duets with the sleep breath
of children, that we might be assured nothing goes unheard,
nothing evaporates, that we could become rocks,
if we only stayed, quiet stone scholars at their feet,
tipping their leaves like books to catch the last chaff light
of a wheat rinsed sky.

And if they were poets perhaps they spoke
of us as if we were our cabin which could not be seen
from the interstates' edge, the same canopy
you sat under on a porch bench, painted your nails
chopped wood to stack beneath the rear eave.
Perhaps they knew of the dinner, you stirred mashed potatoes
with your fork until they were like fresh dirt
in the rain while we argued over where your grandfather
was buried, heard what we could not through the tight
gum glue which kept the doors hinged, the house erect.

Perhaps the next morning it was they who warned us,
the smell like a fox hole hiding its red tailed corpse, an early owl
puffing triplets from a bough, before we found the car
upended against a tree, its contents, the once green
                                        spaghetti-strap shirt
ripped, slung from a sapling like a loose, red, autumn leaf,
the bird's chirp still loud, the sun unchanged
since we left the house. There was not much we could say.

You rode your bike. You tell me you heard only that whir,
the rear wheel rubbing against the frame, a bit of the blue
paint shelling off in the miles of crisp heat
between ten and noon and all the slants of light slicing
the asphalt through the thick wood's inflexible arms bent
in above the street on both sides. You did not see one car,
you told me you did not see anyone until you reached the station,
your bike spurting dust, that you did not faint,
but you don't remember more than "A woman, a young girl."
I was sitting by the road when the ambulance arrived,
your bike strapped to its roof with red cord like a haphazard
antenna, a crashed spindle satellite. That evening: the front porch,
the woods sweeping back we drank beer, you sat on the plaid
stitched chair, I on the swing, the air: warmth-thick with
                                        dim weight,
we heard the last owl I can recall. We spoke about moving.
The house became like a wooden candle, a wax fireplace.

Chris Helms

Agape

It is time for a death cult, America.
In the ancient streets at dawn
come bombs, comes waste
in the water where we pray
in our halos lit with shrapnel.

The face of g-d is rigid and pale,
riding into town like John Wayne
on a clockwork horse.
There is no excuse for peace,
America, licking at the dew
of the Eastern lotus
is for the weak this year.
We got our guns cocked hard.
There are people to kill,
corporate takeovers to plan.

Concrete mausoleums pour
bodies from their mouths
in the South under burning floods.
Ghosts twist from the sky
and raze land bare.

A disembodied hand twitches
angelic, sweat-palmed
on the flashing red button of our brains.
Push it, the skin is light and rapt.

Push it, viscera is coiled
like a snake in a nest.

Oh dear preacher pope
loving presidential America god,
It's too late to be trying
(look pretty). It's too late to be
(spend money). We got angry mouths to feed
force choke freedom to, we got women
to tell what their moral bodies do,
and we got one Good Book
that tells us all the law we need
to lay down.

Secrets are safe
black flies in the walls.
Honor is a code now.
Justice is doing strip shows in the mall.
Thought is the demon, lay down.

I need cameras on the streets.
I need bars on my doors.
I need a 70-inch wide flatscreen plasma
with picture in picture in picture
to watch every sitcom
tragedy reality romance drama
sci-fi fantasy western news report
ever rewritten.

I need black oil for my SUV.
I need a double cheeseburger.
I need a triple caffeine
mocha latte with soy milk
so I can stay up all night
driving to my next job interview.

I need a pacifier smoke,
I need a numb alcohol pain.
But, only doctors push
the best drugs,
and don't you know hospitals
are the new prison,
and in the afterlife of gunfire
morphine needles are just
the longest part of the vein?

CHRIS HELMS

Pop Star Publicity Riot

Tonight on Fox News the revolution
will be televised. We are selling
T-shirts and looted DVD players
on eBay. Come get your commemorative
bric-a-brac, come see the horde
in the streets and we'll give you
five dollars for each scar received
from interracial police brutality.

This is the riot of being
home alone, doing nothing
to save your self. Grab a shotgun
and defend what you love
from everyone you
were told to love last week.

I thought I knew who I was—
another voice in the rising
din of dissent, an individual
for mankind's unrelenting need—
but now I understand my body
is probably just another place
to keep a hot bullet
on its way into a crowd
sleep-walking through
display windows with bricks
and signs in their hands.

All we have to take away
from the authorities
is what they're selling us.

But it doesn't matter,
they'll still try to sell you the fist
you smashed into your neighbor's jaw
for walking into your house.

They'll sell you the gun
you'll have to keep loaded
under your pillow
while you sleep—every siren
you hear in the night
just another boat
sailing us into slave-trade.

This just in: two men found
dead again, a small child
stolen, caves are collapsing
and the rescue team
is digging several holes to fit
cameras into, whatever you're
eating right now is poisonous,
certain animals are carrying
certain diseases that may make
you certainly paranoid,
the government is giving businesses
billions of dollars for stealing yours,
blacks and hispanics are moving
into your neighborhood,
terror is at an all time high.
And now a word from our sponsors.

LIAM WATTS

A Price in Every Box

A suitcase was an embarrassing container for the evil of the world, but it was all Pandora had in her apartment to store him in. The wheels on the suitcase broke off when she got it nearly to the first landing of her apartment building. While they weren't a great help, the plastic rollers had for a while helped her round the top of each step.

She pulled and strained halfway to the second landing when Craig from 3C ascended into view and offered a hand. Craig was annoying, crude, and every afternoon when they passed in the foyer he would give his latest unasked for assessment of what was helping the country descend to hell in a hand basket. Fearing what she would have to gift him in increased attention in return for his assistance, she reluctantly dismissed his offer to help her—but he would have none of it. With a smile and a grunt Craig grabbed hold of the bottom of the suitcase and helped lift the container to Pandora's fourth floor landing. He gave her a wave and a "Have a good day," and flitted back down the staircase whistling a cheery tune. Craig: still annoying, though now *differently* annoying.

Craig was just the latest in a disturbing trend she noticed. An hour after evil's capture and already things all around her started to seem different. She realized she hadn't heard a car horn in quite some time, the constant buzz of people yelling at each other from open windows had transformed to the bleat of compliments and well-wishing, and the only time

136

she heard a siren it was followed by the laughter of children the cop had been entertaining.

She had been searching for evil, for him, how long now? So long she couldn't recall. In fact, there were several decades in there she had even forgotten her search altogether. But she finally remembered earlier this year, after she dumped her latest boyfriend (and it was she who dumped him, don't let him tell you any different) when her existential angst led to her realize she had been asleep on the job.

It was a lucky break when she found him conveniently down the block from her apartment, across from the Fifth Street deli she ate much too many carbs in. And now it sat in a scuffed Samsonite, leaning against her apartment door. She didn't give much thought as to why he, it, evil personified was in the city, her own city, on the same block that she took her morning jogs down. But if there was anything "Uncle" Zeus had constantly scolded her on, it was her thoughtlessness. Now she would show him, she thought.

She got evil . . . him, it (she always did have problems with what to call it, him, since he liked to change shapes and genders at a whim—one of the reasons recapturing him after she released him from his golden cage had proven nearly impossible) across her threshold and unceremoniously plunked the suitcase on its back in the hallway. She latched the three locks on her door, even though she realized it probably was no longer necessary. Pandora sat on the deep walnut-brown wood floor next to the suitcase. He hadn't made a sound all this time since Pandora accosted him on the street, which she found quite odd. No complaints, no bargaining, no threats. She knew he was the master of trickery and deception, so she couldn't quite understand why he put up no fight and didn't attempt to trick his way out of this.

Unless, his silence *was* a trick.

Pandora fingered the diminutive silver padlock that bound the zippers together. She should check, just to make sure he was in there. Maybe he'd escaped. Maybe somehow he had swapped something else in his place at the last second and she never realized. She imagined flinging open the suitcase to find a fire hydrant or a potted plant or a flood of endless joke spring snakes. She had to know . . . *had* to make sure . . . .

The matching diminutive key found its way home, she started to turn it, expecting the dry *chunk* of the lock popping open—when the ring of the telephone snapped her out of the trance. She pocketed the key with a glare at the luggage, blaming it for being inherently cruel to her overactive sense of curiosity, and padded to the telephone in the living room.

"Where is he?" the fierce and earnest voice on the other end immediately demanded.

"Who? What?" She was still somewhat addled from her earlier reverie.

"You know I know when he's contained; we're bonded."

"Skathi? How did you get my number?" Pandora was rattled: The women of the Norse pantheon always intimidated her. Her fellow Olympian immortals were generally haughty at best and passive-aggressive at worst. The Norse were normally just aggressive.

"Like I can't use Information?"

"But I'm not—"

"I called Nezha, alright?"

God, Pandora thought. *I go out with the guy for one decade and ever since he's still stalking me, keeping track of me—and everyone knows it.* She was equally bothered by the fact that Nezha only semi-stalked her, from afar. If he was forward about it, creeped around where she lived, she could have called in a favor and have him smote. As it was, he was just her long-distance snoop. *I have got to stop getting involved with tricksters!*

Speaking of which, Skathi reminded her, "Ever since that issue with Baldr, Loki and I have been psychically connected. I know when he's bound, and I know when he's roaming the world." Pandora actually felt sorry for Skathi, despite the goddess's ire. Skathi was also someone who tended to fall for the bad boys and get herself into trouble. She wasn't bonded to Loki just because of Baldr; she didn't *have* to be involved with Loki's punishment for killing Baldr. No, Odin had been pissed at her for breaking the heart of his daddy's-boy son, Heimdall (Heimmy to all those who liked to see him get all worked up and in a snit, which was daily) by dumping him in favor of Loki, who ended up breaking *her* heart in turn.

"Why do you think *I* have him?" Pandora asked. She held the phone to her face with both hands. "There's any number of deities and demi-gods who have it out for him. Loki's upset a lot of people over the millennia."

"Because you're the only one compelled to actually find him. You know everyone else has come to the agreement that total jerk-wad bastard or not, the mortal world's better off with him free."

That kind of stung. It was true that since the day Pandora released Loki from the cage and thus allowed him to infuse the planet with his evil and wickedness, she had been marked by the often embarrassing obsession to capture him. (Embarrassing because she was pitifully pathetic at the task of tracking him.) Granted, she had that period where the obsession was more of a nagging feeling that she'd forgotten something or had to be somewhere she couldn't recall and was ten minutes late—but even an immortal obsession can get kind of old after a few centuries.

"That can't be true. What about Odin? His precious Armageddon can't happen without Loki locked up."

Skathi sighed. "That's 'Ragnarök.' And you know the dirty one-eyed codger's been missing since Arbor Day, fifteen-sixty-three." Pandora recalled something about a disagreement regarding an old god-folk's home from which Odin was last seen ambling away as his kids threw spears and lightning and lightning-spears at each other. "Plus, unlike some god's End Day Party, Ragnarök's not actually a good time for the geezer."

"Well, I know Apollo would—"

"Don't mention that jerk's name around me!"

"What? Apollo may have moved on after I let Loki out, but I know he still cares about him."

"That narcissistic prig couldn't care about his own mother. Sister. Whatever! You know, you Hellans are a freakin' sex crazed incestuous lot. Makes me sick."

"Look, just because you and Loki had a thing and then he and Apollo hooked up, isn't Apollo's fault."

"He made Loki his bitch."

Pandora couldn't help it, "Skathi, Loki can change into whatever he wants."

"You know what I'm talking about! Masks and whips and cages. Disgraceful, to treat one of us that way."

"'One of us'?" She switched the phone to the other ear and ground a knuckle of her other hand into the endtable. "Skathi, I have a feeling you're not talking about 'us' as in 'us immortals.' I know for a fact some of you frosties are into the alternative lifestyles. Take Foresti: I'd heard he's not all straight and narrow as he puts on."

"You leave him out of this!"

"This is a racial thing, isn't it? You can't stand the idea that your precious Loki, whom you've never gotten over, would dare to be in a relationship with one of our dirty lot. You know, you're a real piece of work, ice princess. Maybe I do have Loki. Maybe I have him stuffed in a suitcase. Maybe he's shoved in there with a forgotten penny, a travel toothbrush, a sock, and you know what? Maybe he *likes* it. What do you think about that, ice princess?"

"You . . . you . . . ." The dark, smoldering rage was palpable through the phone line. A quality ever so literal when the person on the other end was a god.

Pandora's flare of bravery and gumption fizzled. "Leave me alone," she said in a cracking voice and disconnected the call. She looked across the room and down the hall at the bag sitting motionless, forlorn.

"I have a feeling this is only just beginning, suitcase."

There were no more calls that day, but early the next morning they started to pour in. Congratulations from the likes of Themis and Brahma (she *thought* Brahma was congratulating her—he tended to be incomprehensible at times, simultaneously mumbling and shouting and holding conversations with himself), death threats from Heyoka and Veles, and calls of concern and pity from Mariana and Artemis.

Pandora always admired Artemis, but felt like the quiet geeky kid sitting at the nerd's lunch table wishing she could sit with Artemis at the table for radiantly talented and popular kids. (Pandora thought the metaphors television provided for emotional angst were the greatest benefit of the invention.) Artemis was never mean to Pandora, and in fact, was always kind and sisterly to her—whenever she noticed Pandora's presence. She was the first to pat Pandora on the shoulder and let her know it was all going to be OK while the others in Apollo's circle of friends and family (that still hung around him) scorned and berated Pandora for making Apollo alternately weep and rail for a week. Everyone suffered while Apollo suffered. Pandora often asked herself "What would Artemis do?" when she was on the hunt for Loki.

Even Yahweh, who tended to petulantly ignore all the other immortals, called her up on the morning of the third

141

day. Although, Pandora couldn't figure out what the purpose of his call was. At one point she wondered if his call was even related to Loki's situation and the resulting peace and happiness throughout the world. After a while of suffering through the babbling and soliloquies, Pandora hung up. He called back immediately. She saw the caller ID display "God of Gods." She let the machine pick it up. He hung up and called back and this time the caller ID scrolled "Not Me, the I Am. Seriously. Pick up." Pandora rolled her eyes and went to finish making breakfast in her over-sized flannel PJ's and baby seal slippers.

The suitcase containing Loki remained in the hall all this time. At first she spent hours watching it, sitting cross-legged on the hardwood floor. Then on a pillow on the hardwood floor. A couple of times she put her ear to the black ballistic-nylon exterior of the suitcase and thought she could hear breathing, but was never certain. She finally had to throw the key to the suitcase's lock out the window. After a lady who had seen it hit the street returned it to her, after having knocked on the door of every apartment on her side of the building, Pandora flushed it down the toilet.

The confusion she had about why "evil" was locked up as Loki was locked up while some of the other baddies were still around nagged at her for a while, but she decided the whole what-god-was-responsible-for-what-thing was more complex than she was able to understand. Besides, last she heard, Set was killed some centuries back and Satan always was just a big misunderstanding. Most of the other so-called gods-of-evil (as mortals understood them), weren't. Not entirely. For example, Dis Pater was pretty good at farming and Hades was, after all, just a bureaucrat in charge of dead people. As Pandora remembered him, he was kind of a mousy guy with a nervous tick. His most evil trait was that horrible comb-over hair style.

Eventually she went on with her daily routine. She would throw a glance at the suitcase as she walked from kitchen to living room with her bowl of cereal for dinner. Or she'd lean her head back on the couch and crane around the corner and see if the suitcase had changed while she watched her favorite television programs: mysteries and the kind of "reality TV" that claimed to show the hidden true lives of ordinary people (a truly guilty pleasure).

Finally, she realized she would have to do something about the situation: television just wasn't the same anymore. Several of the cable networks disappeared, the news channels that remained only portrayed touching stories of heroism and generosity, commercials (both the clever and the banal) that sold stuff went away, and reality shows that weren't pulled with an announcement from network management that they were "just too exploitative of people" became tediously boring. This had to stop.

When her distant friend, Eris, called her, Pandora took the opportunity to ask her out to lunch. Eris sounded as though she had expected the request: "Of course, dear. I figured you could use some advice." They met at Dozio's and took a table alfresco.

"Eris, I just don't know what to do. I mean, it's been my goal, my job, to find him, for . . . god, forever. And now that I have, I don't feel the least bit relieved or like I accomplished anything. I feel like, like I can actually feel the weight of the suitcase in my hall weighing on *me*. Even here, away from there, I feel it. It doesn't feel right."

"Hon, it's because it's *not* right." Eris sat across from her, stirring a cloud of actual sugar in her iced tea—not one of those unnaturally soft powders from a pastel-colored paper envelope. Eris wore a stylish and expensive, but quite conservative and plain, outfit and equally expensive and understated sunglasses. Her blond hair glowed in the sunlight

143

more than it naturally should have, and made Pandora feel out of place with her t-shirt and cardigan sweater and dark hair pulled back in its usual ponytail. As long as they had known each other, Eris enjoyed a certain ability to radiate beyond her radiant attire while Pandora couldn't seem to do anything but be plain and unnoticed. Despite the differences, the two of them were friends ever since Pandora's first birthday (which, unlike humans, Pandora got to attend fully grown) when Eris pulled Pandora away from the throng of chiton wearing fuddy-duddies and psychopaths, and taught her the art of slingshotting grapes across a room, unseen by your victim.

"How do *you* mean it's not right?" Pandora picked at the spinach and artichoke dip with a triangle of pita bread while Eris took tiny and thoroughly enjoyed bites of apple crumble.

"Look around. The problem with your daily shows is just a symptom of the problem." This was sounding familiar to Pandora. "Look at this place." Pandora scanned around at the faux Spanish décor and happy, babbling people around them. "Have you noticed anyone receiving a bill for their meals? Anyone paying their bill?"

"Hmm, no, I guess not. But I haven't been looking, really. There's a lot of tips on the tables, though."

"You haven't been out much the last few days, have you, dear?"

"Well, not really."

"Money is worthless. No once charges anything; no one is paying anything. The entire world's economy is running right now, as we speak, via gratis and barter."

"What about the huge tips?"

"A gesture only. Finally it's a sincere and non-compulsory gesture, tipping. But *only* a gesture as that paper is no good as legal tender. Goodness, even legality, laws, are irrelevant anymore. No one is breaking any, since no one even wants to."

Pandora smiled coquettishly, "I thought it was the *love* of money that was the root of evil."

"Bollocks." Eris examined a piece of shimmering apple on the end of her fork. "This is really good. Are you sure you don't want a bite?" Pandora shook her head. Eris shrugged and continued after relishing her bite of mid-day desert: "Panda, dear, what is money itself but a symbol of the distribution of wealth. What is wealth? The abstraction which separates the humans between the haves and the have-nots. Upper class, middle class, working class. Even the lower class have more wealth than entire villages in countries previously unknown to most of these mortals. When you locked up evil, you eradicated the concept of wealth and who has it. Did you know that right now, with the mental barrier of money out of the way, more people and food and supplies are flooding into those disease-and-hunger infested areas of the world? Without money to limit people, make them feel like goodness and charity are only possible within the confines of a set and defined dollar amount, people are free to be completely egalitarian, generous. Unfettered charity."

Pandora scowled into her ice tea, no sugar, no lemon . . . please no lemon (they always forget—although not this time). "I . . . correct me if I'm wrong, but isn't that a good thing? I mean, isn't this what they mean by 'heaven on Earth'?"

"Is it?"

Pandora chuckled, "Oh don't do that."

"Yes?"

"That whole answer a question with a question. When did you get your psychiatrist's license?"

Eris smiled and carefully blotted the corners of her mouth with the cloth napkin. "I'm serious, Panda, dear. Ask yourself, is it better or not?"

"Well, sounds like millions of more people living, thriving. I guess no wars, or crime."

"And no egotism, pride, desire, or ambition. Without war, chances are no sonar, GPS, MRI imagers, the Internet. Without ambition, no great American novels. No discovery of the South Pole or any humanity-inspiring acts of courage and bravery. Without desire, art, music, poetry would be significantly less inspirational and compelling."

"You can't be certain of any of that. You can't know any of that won't, wouldn't, be done without the bad side of humanity."

"Perhaps." Eris leaned back, hanging an arm over the back of the chair. "But do you want to take that chance?"

"Even if it doesn't, is that so bad for them? So they don't have a Mount Everest littered with discarded oxygen bottles and power-bar wrappers. They don't have the Mona Lisa. They'll have peace and . . . ."

"And over-population until pandemics wipe most of them out." Eris swung her arm back and hit the person behind her in the side.

The man turned around in his chair and smiled, "Oh, sorry."

"Eris," Pandora replied, "you're not seriously suggesting that the world needs wars as population control."

"Yes, but that's only a part of the need for humanity to have their whole nature returned." She swung her arm back and smacked the man again. The man turned, smiled sincerely though a little confused, and apologized again. Eris continued, "Without ambition and desire they may just accept the nature of . . . nature, and continue providing aid and charity to each other while they wallow in death and misery, smiling all the while." She smacked the guy again. Again the guy turned, laughing as if he were a part of a grand joke, and apologized. "No eventual push into space, allowing this mortal race to survive the destruction of this cradle. No evolution of the species into an exciting and unimaginable posthuman unknown."

"Plus," Eris added, "I like the Mona Lisa. She reminds me of you." She smacked the guy again. Now everyone at his table started laughing and play-smacking each other.

Pandora smiled at Eris, but felt sad and a little disgusted by the simple, innocent love zombies at the next table. She had to lower her eyes. "So, what do I do?" she asked quietly.

"As I always say, dear, 'everything in moderation.'"

Pandora looked back up from under her eyebrows, "*When* do you *ever* say that?"

"Why, when it's to my advantage, of course." Eris popped the last bite of rich, golden apple crumble into her treacherously demure mouth.

With the help of Eris' three-hundred pound bear-like driver, Package Loki was loaded into the trunk of the black sedan.

"I'm proud of you, Panda, dear," Eris told her as they stood on the sidewalk. The early evening air started to cool, and Pandora wrapped her sweater around herself. "I would have certainly expected you to have opened the suitcase by now. After all, it only took two hours for you to open his cage after being warned not to at Apollo's soirée." She looked wistfully at the gray sky. "Seems like eons ago."

Pandora playfully nudged her friend, "It *was* eons ago."

"And I don't look a day older, do I?" Eris chuckled at her own joke, told in some variation or another at every visit of hers. Pandora smiled.

Then she said, "You know, not to be ungrateful for your helping me out here, but somehow I get the feeling that you're taking him more for your own enjoyment than any real desire to help humanity."

Eris gasped. "Child, I'm insulted that you would suggest I would do anything purely for the sake of altruism! It's as if you didn't know me at all." Her driver, having gotten everything situated, stood, impassive and impressive, with his hands clasped in front of him, next to the rear passenger door. "It just so happens everyone gains in this situation, despite my better nature. Can I be blamed for unlucky accidents?" She playfully nudged Pandora back.

"So you'll let him out in short sessions?"

"Twice a day for one hour each, when he's good. Leashed, of course. I may hobble him and allow him to serve guests now and then. That should be good fun, especially when Golden Boy is among the guests. I can see his twisted self-righteous mug already."

"Hmm." Pandora looked down the street. No cars— only bicyclists and pedestrians. She wondered what evil in moderation will end up looking like. "I'm curious, though, why he never said anything."

"What's that, dear?"

"These last few days. No tricks, no conniving. It was almost like he walked into my life after centuries of being a myth to even me, and waited passively for whatever was to happen . . . happen."

Eris gently took Pandora's hands in her own. "Panda, dear, being a one-trick pony gets wearying even for us avatars."

"Yeah, I think I know what you mean."

Eris smiled at her friend. "Goodbye, dear. Promise you'll visit soon."

They kissed cheeks, and Pandora replied, "Promise. Be sure to take care of the little guy."

"Oh, honey, nobody's in better care than in Mistress Eris' hands."

The driver opened the sleek black door for her, then went around to the driver's side. Pandora stood, ends of each sleeve bunched up in her fists, and watched as the car bolted from the curb, causing several pedestrians to jump out of the way and bicyclists to crash in comedic piles of limbs and spinning tires and shouted apologies. She waited to make sure there didn't appear to be any seriously injured innocent souls, and then went back into her apartment building, passing whistling Craig on his way out. She absently hoped the short sessions would be enough to inspire the return of her reality shows.

SATARAH WHEELER

Healthcare City

There's a public bus that stops
right outside my building. It beeps
slow and sharp when it comes to a stop
every thirty minutes until two a.m.,
shrill and even like a pulse machine.

 I dream of hospitals all the time.

Of wheeling my IV stand with me forever,
struggling to change the bags when my medicine
starts to empty, then an hour later, my saline drip.
So unqualified and drawing attention from
everyone on the street when the alarm
on the machine never stops because
I don't know how to make it stop.

I cannot pay to have the needle taken out of my arm.

I wear my paper dress even
when it's cold out, people passing
see my heart inside beating slightly off
and pushing clear liquid in my arteries,
looking at my bare feet
and my chapped white lips
blending into the skin of my face.

The wheels get stuck in the cracks
in the crosswalk halfway across
the street when the light turns green.
People stare at me as the snow
falls into my hair making me
white white
like the walls of the hospital I've left,
but I'm not mad at them.

I know they don't understand.

There are no hit songs played
on the radio about this,
no bestselling novels written
about this.

Just as the snow is sparkling
in my eyelashes and the bags
of medicine are starting to freeze
I make it back home.
I pull my monitor up the stairs
and as the snow melts out
of my paper gown and drips
out of my hair I reach under
the couch cushions feeling for change
and hoping to find a hundred thousand dollars.

I find sixty four cents and drop it into
the empty plastic butter bowl that sits
on the table by my bed. I finally lay down,
the machine beeping and reminding me
and reminding me
and reminding me
that I can't live this way much longer
and I can't pay for a better life.

SATARAH WHEELER

Someone You Think You Might Know

You're an American girl, hung out to dry on a wire between
the Empire State Building and the Chrysler Building,
                                        dropping pennies
onto the sidewalk from stories up, just missing everyone.

They won't kill anyone below, that's a myth and you know it
but better to keep them safe, like houses lined up on a cul-de-sac,
picket fences like front yard scars of stitches sewing front
                                porches to quiet streets.

Your change purse is an absurd replica of the American
                                        flag, your pennies
lying dead in the bottom, gleaming in the sun like the
                                skeletons of these buildings,
shiny steel skulls and guts of businessmen hanging in the
                                coat closets by their ties.

From here you can see someone you think you might know
                                        walking
in front of a record store in Queens, but no.
That's just someone you wish you knew if you had time for
                                knowing.

But oh, the way the clothespins clamp your shoulders to the
                                        twine and your feet
dangle 102 stories above Pennsylvania, above Connecticut
(you can see all of New Jersey hanging here) . . .

you don't mind being alone up here, humming Elvis
                                        Costello, dumping
your change purse, watching it spill out like ugly brown leaves.
Below they are using up your luck; they'll never think to
                                        look here.

SATARAH WHEELER

The Sun, the Sea, and the Small Things We Know

I. Purity
When I was very young, big orange flowers grew on a bush
in the yard, they looked like suns.
I ate the petals smearing dusky pollen on the corners of my
lips and I threw them up as soon as the streetlamps came on.

II. Exigence
I've seen my guts lit up with contrast in my veins on
machine screens named with numbers. Lying on an
operating table barely awake as a man in powder blue put
tubes in my arms and legs.
 Is that me? I wondered
out loud,
looking at the sternum,
          the ribs,
                    the clavicles,
                              the spine
glowing on the monitors.

Yes. The man pressed the plunger on a long needle and
stuck it in my thigh, and it felt sparkly like constellations. I
watched the screen and marveled how congruous my bones
were. Exactly the same on both sides.

Hospitals are dead museums . . . I only half pronounced the
                                          words

as the constellations shot
c o m e t s a n d s h o o t i n g s t a r s into my lips . . .

His face never changed, not his eyebrows, not even his chin
out from under his surgeon's mask, *I don't know what that means.*

I smiled,
      or I think I smiled,
            or I was just still, calm
as he stopped for a moment glancing in the direction of my
                  eyes . . . *I don't either, it's a song.*

He nodded a little, or the earth moved up and down a little,
                  Well, you're not going to die.
A breath of laughter puffed out of my mouth and on the screen
my
ribs
shifted.
How do you know? You never asked how I was feeling.

He pressed a button on the I.V. drip and squeezed the bag a
little, *How are you feeling?*
        My vision swam as I fell out of the stars
            and into the sea,
           saline thick in my mouth
           . . . *Symmetrical.*

III. Novel
Once, in Virginia, in the whitest hotel bed I've ever slept in,
                      I woke up
when the sun burned in through the curtains, and there in
                black was someone new;
a different shadow against sheets with different arms,
                  perpendicular

with mine, intersecting at our wrists. I closed my eyes and
                              there on the lids, we were on a grid with
arrows for our hands and I was X and he was Y—and we
                                        chased each other
to infinity, never getting there and never touching again.

When I sat up, he didn't even stir and I leaned over and wrote
on the stationary *this is one of those moments I'll need to remember*
                                                          later.

IV. Deliverance
Some people are born with valentine hearts
bright red for their passion,
grabbing the world with their fingertips in its neck.
All wrong for everything,
empathy burning like roman candles
and souls like yellow flower petals scraping
across the sidewalk in the Atlantic breeze.
And one day, those people will fill the holes
in the big city crowds and minutes will pass
and we can all be pure again if we try.
The seas can mean more than separation
and our hearts can mean more than biology,
handkerchiefs our breast pockets
yellow for the sorrow, like the sun.

WARREN HAYES

Tale of the Stowaway

After Wallace Stevens

We took a boat out on the lake,
two men, one oar, motor shot.
I sat at bow, he rowed from stern,
the vessel zagged over glass.

The budded limbs of April eighth
drooped spindles in the navy light,
hung hushed, as were our words.
The oar kept watery pace.

A flock of geese arced overhead,
and graced down to the lake.
Their ripples lapped the crusted hull,
when faint scratching caught our ears.

He raised the outboard's wooden lid,
compartment packed with rotten foam.
A field mouse sat staring back
at two men in a boat on the lake.

WARREN HAYES

Cartography

I was seven when my father
brought home the color-coded globe,
the Soviet Union stretching great
orange arms over two continents,
the bumps of the Himalayas, the Andes.
Bored in class, I copied the images
from memory, placing Spain in Scandinavia
and drawing land beneath the North Pole
where Santa surely lived. I asked
classmates their favorite continents—
always Antarctica, because the penguins
were there! But I wanted Europe
and Charlemagne's castles, the chivalry
and crusades that played out in my mind
like recent history. By sixth grade
I wearied of tag and kickball
and carried a notebook to recess instead,
penciling shorelines and islands,
pretending the wide-rule were lines
of latitude. The Americas and Caribbean
lay distorted under my skilled fingers
and I'd date the map 1723, crinkle
the paper into a ball and then flatten
it out again. "Mar del Nort" and other
scraps of crude Spanish
for place names. The clap on my back
from Cortés, Magellan's half-grin.

Last summer I bought an old atlas,
a garage sale bargain. Years later
but my fingers found their stride.
Ontario, Brazil, and India sketched
on college-rule, my mind freewheeled with
walking Parliament Hill, Villa-Lobos plucked on acoustic,
and wise Ganesh with his elephant's head. The weight
of forged memories to fill up those missing places—
the aching plainness, the landlocked
smallness of my Missouri home.

APRIL STUBLEFIELD

Willow Springs Holds Food 'n' Fun Forest Day Again

Sunlight drifted through the once congested street
that day to pass the gathered goods faded by old.
Revived as flying dust, stray trucks, allowed,
a hidden wave of skirts with dancing feet
expanded into table shapes again. Some sold
trinkets brought out from corners. Un-shrouded,
patchwork music rose to chaos with a beat,
a fitting scene for moving time. Feeling bold,
someone built the highway around the town.

Someone built the highway around the town,
a fitting scene for moving time. Feeling bold,
patchwork music rose to chaos with a beat.
Trinkets brought out from corners un-shrouded
expanded into table shapes again, some sold.
A hidden wave of skirts with dancing feet
revived as flying dust. Stray trucks, allowed
that day to pass the gathered goods faded by old
sunlight, drifted through the once congested street.

APRIL STUBLEFIELD

Three Years Later

It rained every day we followed the worn trail
deeper south on sinking man-made pillars
rich with aquatic parasites,
to a land saturated with the gulf's salty tears.
The city was full of cries living
in highway tents. We worked for a week,
cooling our faces in the wetness outside,
decorating ourselves with wildflowers
growing along the levee, placing them
in goggle straps for a picture. Stairs in that wall
led to gray water, waiting. We looked down
on naked houses where the waste lived stagnant
after three years, brown lines staining the walls
eight feet high, a little more each year.
We counted red X's on every other door,
always losing.

APRIL STUBLEFIELD

Star-Shaped Shadows

A breeze of smoke like heavy rainbows
escaped battle on the driveway, blowing out
from star-shaped shadows on the ground.
Our parachutes exploded in the air
to expose plastic soldiers floating
high in the trees, above the reach of family.
Sought by shaking limbs, no victory came
from above, but plastic armor clung still,
cheaply to the chute that wouldn't give.
The singed and whiplashed soldier lost
the fight against the brightening moon rise
blurring lines. As darkness fell to cover
littered eaves, forgotten men, and hide
the blackened streets, abandoned trash,
a flaming celebration filled the sky.
We gave our land a fetid smelling breeze
and left our soldiers hanging in the trees.

D. GILSON

Driving to Dallas

Laura, Anna, Jenny, and I drive
through the wasteland that is Oklahoma

with its Will Rogers and world's largest
McDonald's and nothing else, really.

We drive into the Texas night
through the flatlands and suburban

sprawl with its shopping centers
chock full of dry cleaner chains

coffee chains Chinese chains
submarine sandwich chains

office supply chains mundane
chains greeting card chains

shoe seller chains and the occasional
liquor chain meant to break the (chain)

that is the shopping center highway
from Tulsa to Dallas.

We check into the Holiday Inn
Express in Frisco nestled between

La Rancho Hacienda and a field
being developed for something

and sleep the drive away on crab-
infested mattresses before eating

our way through the continental
breakfast of hard-boiled eggs scrambled

eggs egg substitute and eggs folded
over a slice of American cheese.

We drive through Dallas and I am scared
all we are is the Gap and presidential

yard signs and Toyotas and reality television
stars but Anna assures me as we drive back

north through the night picking up thin
crust pizzas at a small town Pizza Hut

we huddle together to eat under the lights
of the dashboard stereo of the hatchback

that we are all just looking for somewhere
to breathe.

Jeremiah Moorhead

Homebrew

Yesterday the glass carboy in the closet
gurgled and belched the smell of yeast
through the whole house—
but today its aroma finally smacks of booze.

We ran, you and I, as soon as we got home last night,
to the room we decided would be dark and cool,
our soon-to-be-born son's closet—
to check on the progress of our Sunday work together.

Staring at the twirling and bubbling,
we were amazed at the activity
in the mix we combined—
much like the kicks in your belly.

ASHLEY WATSON

On My Father's 14th Year Cancer Free

He stood on the salty sand
looking out into the gritty ocean,
watched his daughter laugh
blissfully as she fed the seagulls
freshly made popcorn,
saw his wife run through
the lightly roaring waves of life.
He sat down on his iridescent
beach towel anxious to rest,
but still wanting one more swim
in the immaculate blue-green water.
He looked understandingly
at the sand crab trying to escape
his fate of the tide, being swept out to sea.

David Hill

Fingerprints

Patrick saw nothing but the netted hoop before him as his hands dribbled the ball back and forth with an almost subconscious precision. His Adidas pounded the cracked pavement as he neared his target. The basketball left his hands in a parabolic arc, swooshed through the net, and returned obediently to his hands as he turned back to an imaginary free throw line.

There was a slight chill to the late October air coming from the nearby pond, and he had long since stripped off his grey hoodie, which lay across the dying shrubs that separated the backyard patio from the grassy field beyond. As he went in for a lay-up, the smacking sound of the kitchen door opening broke his concentration only enough to make the ball touch the rim as it successfully dropped through the hoop.

"Dinner's gonna be ready in about twenty minutes," his mom's voice reminded.

"Yeah," he didn't even look in the direction of this news.

"Patrick?"

"What?"

"It's getting cold out here." This was her best shot at subtlety.

"Uh-huh."

"I don't want you catching a cold."

Was there a mother somewhere who would? "Yeah, me neither."

He heard the door finally slide shut as he continued practicing. Twenty minutes later, he was seated before a foil-covered casserole dish with his parents and his brother Brian.

"Patrick?" his mom tried to make eye contact. After a pause he met her gaze. "Could you put that away now?" She motioned to his ears. He slowly removed the earbud headphones and switched off the MP3 player lying in his lap. His mom led them in prayer and then began portioning out the hot food to each of them.

"Did you pack yet?" she asked, handing him a plate full of chicken and rice.

"Yeah, it's done."

"I was reading the list of things to bring," she continued, "and it said 'no CD players, iPods, cell phones, or video games.'"

"I know."

"God, what are you going to do all weekend?" Brian shook his head with a bite of food between his teeth.

"Not practicing for try-outs, that's for sure," their dad muttered.

"It's just for a weekend," his wife offered.

"A weekend's important if he wants to play on our team."

"Well, I think it will be good for him, and besides, Jill is gonna be there." She smiled at Patrick, as if to say, "I'm on your side." Instead of smiling in return, he busied himself with his meal. His dad and brother seemed to accept her last point, or at least that is what Patrick gathered from their silence.

After dinner he drove with his mom sitting beside him in the passenger seat. He had gotten his driving permit a couple months before, and he was well on his way to getting in the required number of supervised hours needed for his license. Still, the nine months separating his sixteenth birthday from the present drive seemed like a cruelly unnecessary obstacle to his freedom. He turned the minivan into the parking lot that divided St. Paul's Parish from the adjacent grade school. Patrick had spent every year since kindergarten inside those walls, with the exception of the past few months, which had been at the public high school in town.

With a Champion duffel bag slung over his right arm, he pushed open the door into the familiar hallway. He stepped across the alternating black and white tiles of the floor, remembering suddenly a private game from grade school where he would only step on white squares or black squares, depending on his mood. Now he could skip at least three tiles in between steps. He could hear voices further down the hallway; he was nearing the cafeteria now. Stepping through the propped doors, he saw Jill straight ahead, talking with some friends. A smile spread across her face as she ran towards him.

"Patrick! I was wondering when you'd get here." She gave him a quick, discreet kiss as she wrapped her arms around him; his arms involuntarily returned the affectionate gesture. "Come here, we were just making name tags."

He followed, tugged by her grip on his wrist, to her smiling friends. His eye was drawn across the room to Kyle, a casual friend who also went to Maxfield High. Kyle played baseball, though they had played a few pick-up games of basketball before. He grinned at Kyle, who was motioning for him to come over.

Their small talk was soon interrupted by Carol, the parish's youth minister, speaking into a microphone held too close to her mouth, where nearly every syllable made a loud pop through the PA system that had been set up in the room. She was in her twenties, and seemed more like a teenager than an adult to Patrick. She had a bubbly attitude and a radiating smile for everyone there. Beside her was a young man who looked about the same age, with curly hair and a short, stocky build. Patrick wondered briefly if he played soccer. The group of teenagers gathered in front of this pair,

169

and at Carol's invitation sat down on the floor; the retreat was going to begin.

"This weekend could be the most important weekend of your life," she was saying to them, "God has brought you all here for a reason, and he is going to do great things if you will only let him."

Patrick sat patiently through this opening monologue as Jill sat knee to knee with him on the floor, slyly holding his hand between them. He was pretty sure he knew who brought him here. Carol continued, finally going over some of the necessary rules for the weekend, including the no electronics rule his mom had been so thoughtful to remind him of. There would be moments of silence, they were told, to reflect on their life and relationship with God and others. Except in case of an emergency, there would be no leaving the school building.

"This is a time to take a step back from the world, and let go of all the distractions that normally fill our lives."

After this introduction, there was praise and worship, and although it was not music Patrick listened to regularly, it was infectious, and he was joining in with the simple lyrics. Some songs apparently had hand motions, which he found somewhat ridiculous, but since most everyone else was doing them, he began moving along with the music too.

After the singing they sat down again; the young man, who had introduced himself as Jeff, told them he was going to share a part of his personal journey with Christ. Patrick tried to listen to what he was saying, but found it difficult. He began wondering if he could sneak off to the gym to shoot some hoops, but he doubted he would find an opportunity to escape.

"Now, we're going to divide you into small groups to discuss what led you here this evening. Ultimately it was God who wanted you to be here, but God often uses other people to work in our lives."

The room was broken up into groups of five or six, and Jill gave Patrick a playful little pout as they were pointed towards separate groups. They were sent into the nearby classrooms adjacent to the cafeteria. Patrick had to smile a little as he realized his group was entering his former kindergarten classroom. Once inside they sat down on the floor in a circle next to the tiny desks; so far, this evening was starting to feel a lot like kindergarten. One of the girls in his group took it upon herself to lead the discussion and sharing.

"Why don't we start with a prayer?" she asked, getting nods all around. Patrick wondered what would have resulted in someone flat-out saying no. Everyone held hands and bowed their heads. "God in heaven, You are so good and so loving. Send Your Spirit here; help us to open our hearts to what You want to say to us. In Your Son's name we pray, Amen."

There was a murmured echo of "amen," and Patrick opened his eyes just in time to see everyone else's heads look back up.

He snuck glances around the room as they began sharing their stories. He could see where he used to sit over by the window, where he would watch the second graders during their recess. He had been sure they got more time outside than his class ever did. Jill sat behind him, and a rumor floated around that she had a crush on him even then, he remembered. For most of grade school he hadn't talked to her; it was just an unquestionable rule that boys and girls did not mix. There had been a few exceptions of course. Michael, who started in fourth grade, seemed to be almost exclusively in the company of the girls, sharing their secrets and giggling at whatever it was they always giggled about. Patrick had laughed with the other boys when once Michael tried to play football with them, and someone remarked that usually they didn't let girls play.

"So Patrick, why did you come on the retreat?" The circle was staring at him now.

"My girlfriend." There was a faint chuckle from the smiling faces that continued staring at him. He took a deep breath. "And you know, I wanted to grow in my relationship with God; all that good stuff."

His peers nodded approvingly, and he felt relieved as they moved onto their next victim. He knew his second response had been a lie.

That night, he squirmed in his sleeping bag on the cold hard floor, listening to the blissful sounds of sleep all around him. The boys had been assigned one classroom and the girls another. The room's desks had been stacked and pushed around the perimeter of the room to make space for the carpet-like spread of sleeping bags that left no place to walk about without stepping on a sleeping form. The room seemed a lot less dark compared to the thick blackness when the lights had first been turned out. His eyes had adjusted, and now a sliver of the moon had risen into view outside the window, casting a ghostly glow into the sleeping classroom.

Lying on his side, his eyes were drawn unthinkingly to the source of the gentle snoring of Kyle, who lay in the sleeping bag next to his. In this light he could just make out the barely parted lips, and the cheekbones surrounded by gentle waves of dark hair. He looked peaceful, he looked—

No. Patrick flipped his aching body to face away from Kyle. Lying on his left side, he saw only the rising and falling back of a large boy whose name he didn't know.

He thought longingly of his iPod sitting in his room on a pile of dirty laundry, where in a moment of compliance he had left it behind as he packed for the retreat. When he wasn't sitting in class or talking to a friend, those tiny white earbuds were almost always firmly lodged in his ear, even as he went to sleep. He suddenly felt the length of the weekend stretch before his mind it its entirety; Sunday afternoon was starting to seem very far away.

The next morning, he found reasons to not approach Kyle. Jill's nearly constant lock on his arm made this easier, and when they sat down for breakfast, he was relieved to see Kyle at a different table. After this, he didn't think too much about it.

The day continued much like the night before, with talks, small group discussions, and songs, which Jeff led with his acoustic guitar. Out of everything on the retreat, he was finding the songs the least irritating. His mind drifted during talks, he had very little he wanted to share during small group time, but he caught himself half enjoying the music.

After lunch, Carol announced they would have an hour of free time before the next talk. They were allowed to go to the gymnasium—really anywhere—as long as they stayed in the building. Most of the teens migrated towards the gym; Patrick was one of the first inside.

The echoing squeak of tennis shoes on the smooth floor was the most beautiful sound he had heard all weekend. He picked up the first basketball he saw lying on the floor, and felt it move in his hands like it was part of him. He made a lay-up at the net, and then another. He felt a hand on his lower back, and he spun to see Kyle's eyes smiling at him.

"What?"

"Easy man," Kyle smirked good-naturedly. "Care if I join you?"

Kyle stood between him and the basket, staring him down as he put his arms up to make a barrier. Patrick went out to the free throw line, and then drove hard for the basket. He leaned his body to the left for only a second, and flew right as Kyle unwittingly stepped out of his way. Kyle was shaking his head, and shrugged.

"This is why I play baseball."

Patrick passed him the ball. "You try it now."

Kyle gave an exaggerated sigh, and tried to mimic Patrick's moves to the basket. Patrick found it almost laughable, until Kyle almost ran directly into him, and seemed to linger, breathing hard way too close to his neck. He let Kyle make it past him to the basket. Kyle glowed as he threw the ball to him, and Patrick prepared for another lay-up. Again, Kyle tried to block his path, but his weight was all on his right foot; all Patrick had to do was fake left and go right, but he didn't. He stopped, passing the ball back and forth between his legs, while Kyle leaned in, closer. Patrick turned a little, still keeping the ball moving. Kyle's chin was almost resting on his shoulder. His breath came in short bursts, and Patrick turned away from him and the basket, the ball still moving in his hands. Kyle reached under his outstretched arms; Patrick could feel his entire torso pressed against his back, and he nearly lost control of the ball, but instead he spun and listened to the swoosh of the net as Kyle waved his arms needlessly.

Making a firm effort to focus, he blocked Kyle's next shot, and pushed past him when he himself had the ball; he didn't let Kyle get any more baskets, and after ten minutes of this, Kyle passed him the ball saying, "Dude, this isn't a real game, this is just for fun."

"I am having fun."

Kyle shook his head again. "You're so serious, man," he smacked him playfully on the arm as he walked past him. "I'm gonna get a drink; I'm exhausted."

Patrick watched him walk away. Kyle was a bit shorter than him, but he had a slightly fuller frame that filled out his t-shirts, especially across the shoulders. He had a carefree spring in his step, even though Patrick knew he must be worn out from their brief game. Patrick quickly shifted his eyes to glance around the gym. There were other small games going on all around him; a volleyball net had been set up in the far corner. He saw Jill sitting on the bleachers, where he assumed she had been observing him and Kyle. Dropping the ball, he trudged toward her.

"Did you have fun?" she asked.

He wondered if she noticed him staring after Kyle. "Yeah, I needed the practice, even though Kyle pretty much sucks."

She smiled at him as he sat down beside her. "I'm glad you came. Do you like the retreat so far?"

"It's alright."

"Just alright?" she looked disappointed.

Damn. "I'm just gonna have to get used to it. It's different."

She acknowledged this with a nod, and then rested her head on his shoulder. He let her, and sat silently watching the other teens expel the built-up energy from the weekend.

"That's where we danced," she said to his neck.

"What?"

"Right there, under the basketball hoop."

She pointed to where he and Kyle had just been. She was right. The previous spring, at the eighth grade mixer, Jill had asked him to dance. He had no good reason to say no, and besides, he knew the other guys would be jealous, since Jill was one of the prettiest girls in their class. It was a bit embarrassing; the only time he was quick on his feet was when holding a basketball. Jill didn't seem to care though, and when he apologized after the song ended, she said she could teach him sometime. He agreed, and they began hanging out after school for really the first time, even though they had gone to school together since kindergarten. He tried to teach her to play basketball, and she taught him some basic steps she had learned in her dance class. Soon there were rumors they were dating, and Jill had happily confirmed these as true.

He turned to see her smiling at him, before putting her head back on his shoulder. He looked out to the gym floor, and remembered the night of the dance. He pictured Jill leading him to the music, and tried to burn this image into his mind permanently. He would call it defense.

After dinner, the teens broke into their small groups again and went off to the classrooms for some more quiet discussion. Patrick could tolerate these, he decided. No one asked him too probing of questions; all he had to do was give vague answers that sounded similar to what everyone else was saying, and he would pass under the radar.

Presently, Jeff stuck his head through the classroom doorway, and told them it was time to return to the cafeteria. They got up, and followed him. He motioned for them to be quiet. The other groups emerged from classrooms as they passed through the hallway back to the cafeteria.

Patrick was surprised by the change that had come over the large room. The fluorescent lights on the ceiling had been turned off, and instead the only light in the room came from some lit candles in front of Carol, who was sitting very still. There was such a stillness in the air, it felt like they were disturbing the peace just by their presence.

"The topic for tonight's talk is you," Carol was saying. "Each of us bears some quality of God; we are made in God's image."

She continued, and Patrick's attention drifted in and out of her words. Because she had entered the room with her group, Jill wasn't sitting next to him at this moment. He saw her looking intently at Carol, seemingly absorbing every word she spoke. This retreat, this is what she liked. This is where she was on Sunday and Wednesday evenings, while he was at practice or pretending to catch up on homework. It was obvious she liked being here; apparently it was not as obvious that he simply didn't care.

"Now I'm going to play a song for you, it's called 'Fingerprints of God,'" she put a CD into the boom box on the floor beside her. An electric guitar riff rushed out of the tiny speakers, as she turned the volume up so the whole room could hear.

> I can see the tears filling your eyes
> and I know where they're coming from
> They're coming from a heart that's broken in two
> by what you don't see

Kyle wasn't the first; it was a thought Patrick didn't like to entertain. But he had fought it; he had always fought it. He thought of Michael, and all the names he had been called and jokes that had been made about him. He wasn't like Michael. He couldn't be like that. His mind jumped back to the night before; he could see Kyle's features again. No, *no*.

> I can see the fingerprints of God
> When I look at you
> I can see the fingerprints of God
> and I know it's true

His dad and brother didn't have these thoughts; somehow he just knew. His brother had dated several girls, even though he was only three years older than Patrick, and he was always staring covertly at girls. As for his dad, Patrick once found some video rentals he was sure his mom wasn't supposed to know about.

> You're a masterpiece
> that all creation quietly applauds

It made him angry; he just wanted to be like them. He was like them in almost every way, and this just didn't fit.

Fashioned by God's hand
and perfectly planned
to be just who you are

He thought about Jill. Yes, he was thinking about her. He imagined touching her in places no one had touched her before. He was on a church retreat, and he thought about his girlfriend naked. He got a smug satisfaction from this, thinking how shocked everyone in this room would be if they knew.

Oh and God's not through
In fact, he's just getting started

But that was the only satisfaction he got. He felt nothing else. His body didn't react at all.

"Now I'm going to pass out some pieces of paper," Carol said when the song ended, "and I'm going to ask each of you to write down something that is burdening you, that is keeping you from living the life God wants you to live. So often there are obstacles in our lives that make us fearful, and we forget just how much God loves us."

She began passing around sheets of paper, pens, and pencils. Patrick took the paper and pen, and stared at it, trying to push from his mind what he knew belonged on that paper. Jeff began playing guitar again, very faintly, the clear notes filling the tranquility.

Patrick held the pen hesitantly; he glanced around him, at his peers hunched over their own slips of paper in the drowsy semi-darkness. He made certain no one could see what he wrote. He shielded the scrap of paper with both his arms, and barely moving his wrist, touched the pen to the paper. He watched the word form as his hand moved. He wondered if he had pressed too hard, if it would leave an etching on the pad of paper he was using as a writing surface, where it could be seen by someone else. There it was.

Carol had dragged a small metal tub in from of them, and set a lighter next to it. "When you're ready," she said, "take that paper, and bring it up here. Whatever the burden is, give it to God; you no longer need to carry it," she finished as she set fire to her own scrap of paper and dropped it into the tub.

The gentle guitar continued across the room, a song Patrick had heard the night before, accompanied only by the rustling of paper and periodic sniffles from the group. Silhouetted by the fire, shadowy figures would get up and kneel by the metal tub, and after a brief pause feed the paper to the hungry flames. Divorces, estranged friendships, abuse, poor grades; all these secret adolescent woes were consumed, as the bearers stood and walked away, freed from their troubles. It seemed somewhat superstitious, but Patrick felt himself drawn to reduce his sheet of paper to ashes just the same.

He prepared to stand. He told himself he would go—now. He didn't move. Most of his fellow teens had already given up whatever it was that was holding them down. He didn't want to be the last one or worse yet, miss his chance to before the lights came back on and they went on to cheerier, less serious activities. He could do this; all he had to do was get up, walk to the tub, and let it go.

He was pretty sure everyone else had gone, and the urgency of the moment motivated his arms to push himself up. Clutching the paper in his palm, he approached the flames and squinted at its flickering brightness. Now before the fire, he knelt, and felt the heat on his face. He saw the charred remains of secrets lying on the metal bottom, devoured and unrecognizable curls of ash. He moved his hand towards the flames, closed his eyes, and a prayer escaped from him, from somewhere he didn't even know, begging God to take the unwanted word and all that was attached to it.

A moment later he was turning back, away from the fire, to return to his place on the floor. The paper was still in his sweaty hand. He wasn't even entirely sure why, but there it was, still rolled between his fingers. Sitting back down, he held it in his palm, and stared at it, wondering if anyone noticed what he had done. He almost felt guilty and deceitful, but he couldn't walk up there again.

Still, it was just a word. He didn't see all the other things that word would hold for him, that also had been spared along with it. He didn't see breaking up with Jill, staying single for the rest of high school, or going to college and waking up alone, after giving himself away to a guy he barely knew. He didn't hear his dad's rage or his mom's cowardly silence when he told them he had a boyfriend. He also couldn't have imagined an ally in his brother, and the resulting familial civil war this would bring. For now, he only saw a word.

The lights in the room switched on. He saw faces blinking in the comparatively harsh light as their eyes adjusted. There was an amiable feeling in the group as hugs were exchanged and people clustered together. He looked around. Faces showed relief and freedom. Patrick watched the flames in the tub, though not as impressive now in the fluorescent light. Having run out of secrets to burn, the flames grew weaker and smaller as he watched. Looking on he felt no regret as he slipped the paper into his pocket.

LAURA REGER

Coffee for Scarface

Sugar and cream in Chicago for the Five Points gang:
Joseph Reger, a young man, ties his black apron
(it's time to plan, Mary Mae, marry me)
around his waist. Sections, A, C, and E today,
but let me wash the blood off my hands first.
It's kind of slow this afternoon—Hello, folks!
Gotta play my cards well, you know,
please, call me Joe—What can I get for you today?
Torrio would have my head if I couldn't pull through,
how about some drinks to start off?
But I'm the Big Fellow now, and it's all about
be nice to them, Joe, no mistaking that face,
putting the salt where the salt goes and
Al Capone, Al Capone, no mistaking that face.
The sugar where the sugar goes, but I like salt
with the whole gang, too, and his woman,
in wounds, that's the best place, sugar
can't mess this up, Joe, can't afford to mess this up or
only goes with you, Mary Mae, 'cause
you'll be a dead man.
You're the sweetest thing in the world. Speaking
hurry, men, hurry! Gotta get these men their food
of salt and sugar, I think I see our food
quickly. Thanks, Steve, that all looks right.
Coming. Yes, they're bringing it now, that
Al Capone, Al Capone, no mistaking that face—
Joe fellow. My, they're prompt. What do you think, gang?

CAROL AUTERSON

Complete Set

Before we married
his mom asked me
what glassware
I wanted, I told her
Ball Mason jars
with handles. Simplistic
and clear, they were
easy to see through. Some
etched with fruit-filled
cornucopia, *Golden Harvest*.
Didn't receive any
for our wedding. She
gave me a sprouting kit
with a wide mouth jar.
Growing bean sprouts
was a novelty. Still sought
a set of drinking glasses.
Found salt and pepper shakers
at the store, nothing
large enough for beverages.
Scanning flea markets,
antique malls, I pieced
together a set of twelve
by the time her son left me.

MEAGHAN YOUNKER

What Is Envy

Not the way she outsmarted me, convinced me
to stand on the curb, thumb out, unaware
and smiling, until a nice someone stopped and told
me to *go inside, little girl.* Or how she brushed
Barbie's blond locks while I combed Ken's plastic
head. Not the way she read chapter books
in kindergarten, the way she never failed
a test, never had to study. Not each time
she traveled to Venice, London, and Paris
for her needed vacation time, not when she sped
through town in her shiny gift from Daddy.
Only the way she smirked, tossed her hair,
don't worry, you can be like me someday
spilling from her perfect mouth.

MEAGHAN YOUNKER

Ladylike

She would have to explain to Mother
why she hated Jimmy Terhune
for calling her Miss Priss during recess,
how he stuck out his tongue and made fun
of her pink ruffled dress, tugged
on the ribbon Mother had neatly tied
in her blond hair, perfumed and curled.

She knew Mother would ask her to explain
the curled fist when she finally punched
Jimmy Terhune in the nose, made blood trickle
from his nostrils, how Mrs. Hewitt scolded her,
Such behavior is not polite for a young lady,
and of course she would have to explain
why she punched Mrs. Hewitt too.

BILL SHULTZ

Café at Close, U.S.A. 9/10/08

Damn,

desolate.

If it wasn't for the jazz in the back room
        I'd be hearing

                                ghosts.

Probably just one

or two
        clinking glasses before drinking

in the quietest moments of the evening before

the endless morning. It begins
                        while we're sleeping,

the shrill shrieks
        after blasts shredding
                        the silence
of a sand-blown afternoon:

One, two, three, four . . .

III. Archival Treasures
from the Ozarks

MILLER WILLIAMS

Unpublished Correspondence:
An Editor's Advice to a Poet

*Founder and long-time director of The University of Arkansas Press,
Miller Williams mastered the art of careful, truthful, useful criticism:
witty and savvy, the following letter (from the 1980s, handwritten on
Press stationery) responds to a fellow poet's request for feedback. Taking
Williams' advice, the poet (no need to name names) turned out a better
collection, indeed, winning an award for several of its poems. We print
the following as a model of critical correspondence and as a testimony to
Williams' benign influence upon American letters.*

Dear ——,

It's a good manuscript; it can still be better. You've
come too far to profit now from my marginal scribbles; the
revisions—small moves—that can take this collection the
next step toward perfection will have to come from your own
good ears and eyes, as they pay attention to every line again.

To give you a start toward that, I gave the manuscript to
my senior editor, a woman with a good feel for a poem. She's
first reader on all the poetry manuscripts that come into
the Press, and she's hard as hell to please. I assigned her the
responsibility of first reader because she bores easily and has
an acute allergic condition—banality and posing cause her
hands to burst into flame. She assumed that the manuscript
was a submission to the Press, and so she read it carefully
and prepared the brief report I've enclosed. It should both
delight and instruct you.

We get a poetry MS a day, or about that; this is the most positive report she's given me in almost two years. Your chances of placing the manuscript with a press as it is are therefore pretty good; if you'll take another close look at the poems, they'll be even better.

Here's what I suggest.

With the editor's comments clearly and consistently in mind, sit down when you have a few unhurried hours and read the poems aloud to yourself—or aloud to someone else, if you know a good, astute reader of poetry who's got the time—and listen and look, line by line, for too bland a sentiment, too flat a talkiness, wordiness, just those things. Try to make every line (that isn't this already) an artifact of conversationality, barely jacked up in energy-level by compression, rhythm, and sound-play. Look especially to making each line a pleasure to the tongue. If you can do this, most all the other elements will take care of themselves.

If you don't do this, you've got a good collection. If you'll do it, you might have a superb one.

Warmly, as always,

Miller

James S. Baumlin
and Lanette Cadle

Portraits of Womanhood in the Artwork of Rose O'Neill

> She was great, rich, vibrant, creatively stimulating; she was *complete* (male and female) . . . . [T]he dramatic contrast between the kewpie and her strong, masculine, mystic, pagan drawings is one of the points to bring out. And yet, Rose was so big in every way that the kewpie was as harmonious to her nature as the *Urmensch* she drew in her "secret" drawings.
>
> —Ted Shawn, "father" of American modern dance
> (McCanse 7; emphasis in original)

> Both my sister and I have studied art in Paris and we have lived in Italy. I suppose it is from there that I formed the resolution that life without beauty is unlivable.
>
> —Rose O'Neill (quoted in the 25 April 1915 *New York Press*)

2009 marks the Kewpie's one hundredth birthday: reason enough to commemorate its maker, Rose Cecil O'Neill (1874–1944), who remains forever wedded to her still wildly collectible popular-culture icon (see Fig. 1). It was at Bonniebrook, her family home in Northern Taney County, Missouri, that she invented the elfin creature whose name was "baby talk" for Cupid. In her obituary, the 6 April 1944 *Springfield (MO) Leader and Press* gives the artist's explanation: "It is a little pet name of Cupid, but there is this difference: Cupid gets folks into trouble. Kewpie gets them out. The Kewpie is a little philosopher, always searching out ways to make the world better, happier, and funnier." Using various media, O'Neill set quickly to marketing the elf-child (female

Figure 1. Rose reclining at Bonniebrook

Kewpies were often distinguished from their fully-naked male counters by a bonnet or apron)—though, as she writes in her autobiography, it was "not until the autumn of 1913 [that I realized] there was a 'Kewpie craze,' the greatest success—I was told—in the history of toys" (Formanek-Brunell 109).[1]

---

[1] Here and elsewhere, we follow Miriam Formanek-Brunell's edition of O'Neill's autobiography and draw amply from her scholarly introduction. Our study also

The Spirit of '76.

Figure 2. Kewpies marching for woman's suffrage, 1915

Writing in the 24 November 1934 issue of *The New Yorker*, Alexander King offers a retrospective on the then sixty-year-old O'Neill's life and work: "made of rubber, chocolate, Bakelite, wood, cloth, and ice cream," the Kewpies "paid adequately for the upkeep of Villa Narcissus in Capri and Carabas Castle in Connecticut" (see Fig. 2). Paid "adequately," indeed: as O'Neill's travelling companion and French teacher, Jeanne Galleron, declared, the Kewpie had made her "at one time ... fabulously rich" (McCanse 8)—a millionaire "captain of industry."[2] And "Rose's boundless

draws on the spade-work research of Vernon D. Jordan, Jr., one of O'Neill's most devoted researchers and private collectors; his many pamphlet-length publications offer windows—delightful glimpses—into O'Neill's life, times, and art (readers interested in Jordan's work might visit his website: http://users.dwx. com/~wings/). Above all, we thank the artist's great-grandnephew, David O'Neill, for access to his collection of O'Neilliana. Housed in Galloway Village (a quaint hamlet to the southeast of Springfield, Missouri's historic town center, which the modern city has grown to encompass), The David O'Neill Collection represents the nation's most extensive gathering of the artist's original sketches, paintings, photography, correspondence, and manuscripts—not to mention the massive ephemera of Kewpie dolls and Kewpie-inspired posters, postcards, cutouts, clothing, china, and suchlike. Beyond these debts, we seek to allow Rose (and her contemporaries) to speak for themselves.

[2] Such is her description in the 20 February 1921 *New York Times* article, "Women Who Lead the Way," celebrating "women who have been successful financially as well as professionally." According to Rose's late nephew, Paul O'Neill, she "made a fortune from the dolls, one company alone paying her $485,000 in royalties" (Ruggles 30). Her Kewpie books and illustrated magazine stories proved as lucrative: an invoice (dated 17 March 1927) from *The Ladies' Home Journal* records royalty payments of $2,100 for a three-month installment of the series, "Kewpieville." Obituaries list her Kewpie-industry revenue at $1,500,000. In 2009 dollars (adjusting for inflation), that figure might be multiplied as much as tenfold.

hospitality," King continues, "attracted new hosts of esthetes. It is a well-established fact that guests invited for a weekend remained two years." O'Neill ranged far afield from her family's Ozarks home, moving (while a teenager) into a New York City convent school, from there to a rented flat in Washington Square, later purchasing a mansion in Westport, Connecticut, and later still an artist's villa on the Isle of Capri; she spent years traveling across Europe (see Fig. 3), always well–attended, at all times "determined to live the life beautiful," as King puts it. Her generous extravagance was, in King's words, "her greatest charm and most fatal indulgence." Falling into penury, she spent her last years in Bonniebrook, "safe from 'the Wolves,' as in later years she called city life, with its . . . ever increasing demands on her already depleted fortunes" (Horine 1). At age sixty-nine, she would pass away in a nephew's Springfield home.

Figure 3. Rose painting at Caradossi's Studio, Paris

Presumably an Easterner, King would have had little notion of the Ozarks' longstanding appeal to artists and writers. In his article, thus, King tries to extend the distance between the Rose of Washington Square and her Bonniebrook homestead. "For a while," King writes, "she contented herself with a mediocre little farm in Missouri located in the neighborhood of her father's chasm"—a description that O'Neill would surely have scorned. Such a setting, King suggests, proved too remote and insufficient for a famous artist and her equally famous, growing entourage. Glancing backwards, King describes her at age thirty (ca. 1904): "successful, beautiful, and surrounded on all sides by unceasing hosannas of adulation," O'Neill "had always had strong Bohemian leanings; that is to say, she had no regard for money, was extremely unconventional, and desperately romantic."[3]

In actuality, Bonniebrook remained a refuge throughout her lifetime, a place for rest and renewed inspiration. In her autobiography, O'Neill describes its purchase: "it was after about twelve years of Omaha and the Nebraska prairies that Papa had bought himself an Ozark brook. . . . The place had been abandoned by a native who had been invited to go to another county for having assisted in the last lynching by the Baldknobbers. . . . We named the place Bonniebrook and fell in love with it for good. We were lost in a legend" (60).[4] So, in one respect at least, King's article gets it wrong: Rose Cecil O'Neill—arguably America's most distinguished woman graphic artist of the early twentieth century—belongs to the Ozarks (see Fig. 4).

In another respect, King's article gets it right: given her "strong Bohemian leanings," O'Neill was "extremely unconventional" and "desperately romantic." He offers no

---

[3] O'Neill's unpublished "Washington Square" diary (she kept similar notebooks at various times and places) records the witty "table talk" at her various soirees and an occasional guest list. Over the years, the names have lost much of their luster, though one guest in particular, Charlotte Perkins Gilman (1860–1935)—author of "The Yellow Wallpaper" (1892)—remains among the most famous and influential feminist writers of her generation. O'Neill's autobiography describes their friendship: "Charlotte Perkins Gilman would come into the Washington Square place, put her arm round me, and say she wanted someone to play with" (116).

[4] The O'Neill family, indeed, was among the region's early conservationists. The 26 December 1916 *De Moines Register* reports the following on the youngest sister, Lee: "plans for help in the conservation of the Ozarks . . . were made this afternoon by Miss Lee O'Neill, artist and sister of Miss Rose O'Neill of Bonnie Brook, Mo. . . . Miss O'Neill told of the devastation of the forests to provide railroad ties, and urged the conservation of the Ozarks as a state or national park. . . ."

Figure 4. Rose at work in Bonniebrook

explanation; presumably, his 1930s *New Yorker* readership would have understood. But, from our distance of years, the O'Neill of King's description has been largely forgotten—as good as lost. In salient fact, O'Neill's artistry reaches beyond elfin dolls and illustrated children's books. In her life and work, O'Neill was an amalgam of apparent opposites: suffragette and high-life socialite, serious novelist and cartoon humorist. Her subjects alternatively low- and high-brow, she moved easily from Jell-O advertisements to fine-art exhibitions in New York and Paris. She was a successful businesswoman in a "man's world."[5] She was also a pacifist during the Great

---

[5] In *Memories of Rose O'Neill*, Maude M. Horine quotes an article from *Puck*, the humor magazine at which Rose won her early fame; accompanied by her photograph, the article declares that "no modern worker, in black and white, ever sprang so quickly into popularity as *she*. Because O'Neill *is a woman*" (Horine 14; emphasis added). The point is simple, yet poignant: O'Neill's earliest readers had no idea that their favorite illustrator wore bloomers. By this means, she established her fame in "a man's world" without suspicion or much prejudice.

War,[6] a drinker during Prohibition,[7] a free-spender during the Depression. Twice divorced (though Irish-Catholic) and childless during an age of feminine domesticity, she lived with her sister while surrounded by admirers and occasional lovers. While still a teenager, she left (without an adult chaperone) for New York City, taking the town and its *literati* by storm; by her twenties, she was the nation's highest paid, most recognizable popular artist. A fellow artist and Midwesterner, Thomas Hart Benton, named her (perhaps effusively) "the world's greatest illustrator" (Ruggles 2); while at the height of her powers, she had few rivals (see Fig. 5).

So, it is not the Kewpie's creator but the "unconventional . . . romantic" whom we seek in this brief essay, and whom we glimpse in her artwork. As we shall argue, O'Neill's "Bohemian" romanticism was reflected in and reinforced by her lifestyle and best expressed through her serious sketchwork and illustrations. Clearly she was complex, in both character and emotions. She did not so much flout societal conventions as reshape them to fit her needs, much as her art foreshadowed changes in American womanhood. Feeling "deeply ambivalent about married life" (Formanek-Brunell 12), O'Neill went so far as to declare herself "withdrawn from marriage" (13).[8] Sharing adjacent Greenwich Village flats—"nests," as she calls them—with her younger sister,

---

[6] Several posters and published poetry reflect her anti-war sentiments. In "Soft Song," O'Neill expresses a women's sensuous antidote to warfare: "After the War / Let us be soft, / Let us not be brave; / Nor put more iron ships upon the wave, / . . . And if one calls, let us no longer come" (1–5).

[7] "To Eric for Hootch—a modest offering," she writes on an envelope (which, we might imagine, delivered some dollars in payment); she signs it, playfully, "from Susan B. Anthony." Clearly, O'Neill saw no necessary connection between suffrage and the women's temperance movement. Though rarely photographed smoking, she indulged in cigarettes and an occasional pipe.

[8] She made this pronouncement in 1907, after the collapse of her second marriage. Throughout this and the next paragraph, quotations are taken from Formanek-Brunell's introduction to O'Neill's autobiography.

196

Figure 5. A study in self-portraiture

Callista (1883–1946), O'Neill challenged "standards of propriety for women in numerous ways" (11).[9]

Not surprisingly, O'Neill was an ardent suffragette, yet she was perceived as "a rebel" even "among reformers" (11), as her readings, conversation, and aspects of her lifestyle hinted at "anarchism, atheism, and free love" (11).[10] While

[9] Formanek-Brunell elaborates: "by preferring her sister to suitors, rejecting marriage as a socially sanctioned institution, and deliberately choosing not to have children, O'Neill was challenging the primacy of the nuclear family and women's role in it" (Formanek-Brunell 13–14).

[10] Her personal library included anarchist pamphlet-literature, while Darwinist evolution becomes an explicit theme of her "sweet monster art." An article in the December 1925 *Woman Citizen* describes these:

> She called them monsters, and [they] belonged thousands of years before a so-called civilization had culminated in a Great War. They were pre-Adamite, half-human creatures, muscular, searching, dumb and instinctive, driven by

in her thirties (again, reflecting the time of King's character-sketch), O'Neill became "romantically involved with a much younger man," a nineteen- or twenty-year-old art student whom she admired for his "strikingly feminine face" (13). As Miriam Formanek-Brunell suggests, "O'Neill was fascinated by androgynous forms and sensitive to the sensuality of women" (13). Perhaps so, but a paradox lurks in this last claim, in that androgyny tends to negate, repudiate, or otherwise reconcile gender-difference, whereas O'Neill's mature art (particularly of the 1930s) celebrates gender and eroticizes the female body, reveling in its beauty and *jouissance*.[11] At the same time, O'Neill's women prove largely indifferent to the so-called "male gaze," rejecting male possessiveness and resisting domestication. More strongly than previous studies, our essay demonstrates O'Neill's adoration of beauty in its various forms, embracing a continuum of gender outside of socially-conservative, conformist views. For, indeed, "life without beauty is unlivable": so O'Neill reminds us (in an epigraph to this essay), and we might take her at her word.

The drawings, posters, postcards, and family photographs preserved in The David O'Neill Collection reveal much about Rose and her vision of "modern" American women and men. A sampling of these materials follows, much of it heretofore unpublished. We seek "to illustrate" Rose's own images with pertinent historical and biographical context; our interpretations, needless to say, remain speculative and open-ended. In what we have written thus far and throughout what

---

desires for which they had neither name nor reason. Roots flowed from the feet of one, chaining him to the still earth. Sentient mountains put forth groping hands and feet, rocks twisted and agonized their way into half life. (Ruggles 22)

[11] *Vive le différence*: Rose needed no French teacher for this particular lesson. Though we keep scholarly jargon to a minimum, our vocabulary here (along with our general method) belongs to the post-Lacanian psychoanalyst and Bulgarian-born "French feminist," Julia Kristeva.

follows, three years (from different decades) predominate:[12] 1904 (when Rose added fiction writing to her artistic repertoire, publishing her first successful novel); 1915 (one of her New York City years, when Rose and sister, Callista, were champions of women's suffrage); and 1934 (a retrospective year, by which time Rose had lost some of her fame, much of her bloom, and most of her money). Though we follow a rough chronology, images have their way of reaching across years, haling their earlier and later fellows; we apologize, thus, for the back-and-forth nature of our narrative. Finally, the images we have chosen reflect three intertwining themes: O'Neill's popular- and fine-art representations of gender; her activities as a feminist and suffragette (including her efforts at reforming women's clothing); and her deep, soul-mate identification with her younger sister, Callista. Besides creating the Kewpie doll, O'Neill reconstructed gender and its cultural/artistic representations.

Let us turn now to the art of Rose O'Neill.

---

[12] In this essay, we defer consideration of Rose's "sweet monster" artwork and her lyric collection, *Master-Mistress*, both products of the 1920s.

I. Women and Men.

Figure 6. A studio portrait of Rose, ca. 1904

The above photograph (we are guessing at the date) shows the pre-jazz age Rose O'Neill sporting what would later be celebrated as a bob haircut (see Fig. 6). As Rose writes in her autobiography, "I cut my hair quite a while before the general cropping . . . . I was always rebellious against harness and hairpins, until time and fashion released my viscera" (100). Exactly how "rebellious" is indicated by the 26 March 1916 *Washington Post* article, "Fair Tresses Are 'Bobbed'":

> Mrs. Charlotte Perkins Gilman . . . has directed more
> and more attention to the fact that more and more

women are cutting their hair short after the manner of men. "It was not the Lord who gave men short hair," observed Mrs. Gilman, "it was the scissors." . . .

Among the well-known women who have challenged St. Paul's declaration . . . are Rose O'Neill, illustrator and inventor of the "Kewpies"; Isadora Duncan, the dancer; . . . and Henrietta Rodman, the most widely known public school teacher in the United States.

Interviewed by an obviously female reporter, Rodman holds up Rose as an example of shorn beauty: "You, with your hair done up, cannot show half as much hair as Rose O'Neill does, . . . with that wonderful lion's mane around her face."

Depicting a woman entering her thirties, the photograph places Rose about the time of her first novel, *The Loves of Edwy* (1904). By then, Callista would have become her private secretary; she would be several years past her disastrous first marriage to Gray Latham (d. 1907)—who reputedly abused her (and her wealth)—and but recently married to her second husband, novelist Harry Leon Wilson (1867–1939). Originally her editor at *Puck* magazine, Wilson—remembered nowadays for his comic western, *Ruggles of Red Gap* (1915)— wooed and wedded Rose in story-book fashion, carrying her off to Europe with several fellow-artists in tow. Though more stable than her drinking, gambling first husband, the staid Wilson soon tired of her "baby talk" (which, curiously, contributed to her invention of the Kewpie). They divorced in 1907, after five years of marriage. From then on, Rose would live husbandless, childless, and unfettered.

As a woman representing women in the then "man's world" of publishing—she was an associate fellow (1914) of New York City's elite Society of Illustrators—O'Neill had a built-in viewpoint that male illustrators of the time lacked. The women in her artwork not only had inner lives that jumped off the page, they had a modern sensibility that was at times predictive of how American popular culture would develop. But while her women may take on modern attitudes or pursuits, they do not reject their feminine eros. They were women in an expanded definition of womanhood, not females trying to be male. Sojourner Truth's refrain, "and ain't I a woman?" comes to mind. They were women all, but women who regularly (and comfortably, without guilt or self-consciousness) stepped outside of conservative cultural boundaries.

Figure 7. Youth must rule

Reminiscent of her early work for *Puck* magazine, this sketch (see Fig. 7) seems a curious throwback to the prim-waisted Gibson-girl fashion that O'Neill rejected for herself. The drawing seems to prefigure the flapper-to-come—the youthful, independent, decorum-breaking "modern" woman of the 1920s. The young lady has just finished painting her nails (symbolically, perhaps, from the inkpot resting beneath her hand). Through the early decades of the twentieth century, nail polish remained a habit for the rich. In her autobiography, longtime *Vogue* editor Diana Vreeland tells of how society women of the 1920s treasured their manicurists, the one who concocted the latest shade or a longer-lasting polish being much sought after (148–149). Rarely could women outside "Mrs. Astor's Four Hundred" take the time or expense to keep up painted

202

nails; O'Neill, however, was a firm believer in beauty for the masses.

And the men in the drawing provide more than background. They form a balding wall of disapproval on the right, which the young man on the left brushes away, his outstretched arm clad in a loud, checked sport jacket. With a newspaper clutched in his other hand, the proud youth smiles approvingly at the lady's efforts. (And the turnip at the top right? The reader's guess is as good as ours.)

Hinting at mysteries, O'Neill modernizes the classical muse of lyric (particularly erotic) poetry (see Fig. 8). Though unseen by the man, an intensely feminine muse dominates both the composition and the composer hunched over his desk. Though the lamp by her face seems to equate

Figure 8. Erato inspiring her man

inspiration with the traditionally masculine "light" of reason, Erato's outstretched hand declares her guiding, indeed controlling force. Rose leaves no doubt: creativity belongs to woman. And Erato— whose name (as Rose knew) means "Beloved" or "Desired"—is very much a "modern" woman in body and soul. Signed "O'Neill Latham," it dates from the time of Rose's first marriage (between 1896 and 1901).

Vanity, O'Neill acknowledges, does not belong to woman solely. In this pen and ink drawing (see Fig. 9)—an illustration for *The Loves of Edwy*—the rich, handsome, semi-villainous Georgie contemplates his image: "the dark aspect that drew the golden woman winks as usual from the glass, and there

Figure 9. Man's brooding narcissism

is no grey in the Stygian blackness of the hair . . . . I am still, in the language of a peddler, 'quite a handsome article'" (12–13). The "golden woman," O'Neill's tragicomic heroine, Aspasia Jane, cannot help but fall "for that barbaric head with the perpetually astonishing blue eye in the black face" (13).

204

In Georgie, it is hard not to find hints of "the debonair Gray Latham, who had posed for many of the young men" in Rose's early drawings (Horine 14). To give O'Neill's first husband his due, Latham was an early pioneer of Edison's kinetoscope technology, directing several early short-films; still, he was content to rely on his wife's staggering income. A reputed gambler, hedonist, and alcoholic, he paid off debts by visiting the various publishing houses personally, collecting O'Neill's royalties "on her behalf."

Figure 10. A dangerous liaison

Like her teenaged heroine, Aspasia Jane, O'Neill fell in love too soon, won over by the dark, dashing, and dangerous Latham. In the drawing above (see Fig. 10; again illustrating *The Loves of Edwy*), Jane stares dreamily off into the daylight, innocent and unaware of her companion's darker thoughts:

[S]mall sign did the little creature give of the treasures she held, that afterward she was with such

heartrending grace to proffer me, and once again
withdraw.

Her hunter was at the very gate, but she did not
cry: "Oh, ominous! He comes to steal my heart!" . . .
(11)

But as the plot unfolds, Jane must choose between Georgie
and Edwy—a self-made man who arrives on the scene like
"the trade wind, blowing steadily one way, like the breath of
destiny" (see Fig. 11). It is hard not to see elements of Rose's
own psychology projected here, as she had herself left one
man (Latham), only to find another (Wilson).

Figure 11. Whom to choose?

Publishing in the 10 September 1904 *New York Times*,
an anonymous reviewer notes the novel's unhappy ending:
"Aspasia Jane, golden in hair and in heart, is the inspiration
of both, but may not save herself or them. . . . In the final
wreck of things the author is relentless to leave sentiment
not a leg to stand on." In a sense, Rose foretells the failure
not of one, but of both her marriages.

Having twice endured divorce, Rose made it a subject of
her mature literary and visual art; still, more than personal
experience, her work reflects the rapidly shifting gender

206

Figure 12. Losing a wife

roles that marked the "first wave" of feminism, in part defining the American twentieth century. Apparently left unpublished, only the title page and an illustration (see Fig. 12) remain from her 1930s short story, "Losing a Wife." On the surviving page, O'Neill gives a dialogue "hook" from the climactic scene—the moment of the wife's declaration, which the above sketch seems to illustrate: "'Are you sure you want to leave me, Leila?' / 'Don't make me repeat it, Charles.' Her voice trembled." The wife is not lacking in compassion, but she maintains her resolve. Her future lurks in the window, handsome, but hardly boding a secure, comfortable life. There is no winner in this scene, no hero or heroine—or even, necessarily, a villain. As he stares voyeur-like through the open window (letting him eavesdrop, as well), the younger rival's face presents an oxymoron of emotions: leering yet nervous, perhaps surprised and unsettled, he may be hearing words that he, too, hadn't fully anticipated. The sudden burden of having "gained a wife" seems a weight upon his brow.

Figure 13. Female beauty displayed

Likely from the 1930s, this drawing (see Fig. 13; numbered "3." in a sequence, of which several survive) presents a pillowed semi-nude woman in a style reminiscent of Alberto Vargas—Rose's popular contemporary, whose long career stretched as far as to an album cover for 1990s rock band, *The Cars*. The glamorous "Vargas girls" were sold as "pin-up" and calendar art, as well as featured in *Esquire* and *Playboy*. O'Neill's own glamour girl is sensuous, yes, but she is also a celebration of health and beauty. ("How can anything unnatural be really beautiful?" O'Neill had declared, back in 1915, to *The New York Press*.) As important, *she exists for herself* rather than for the (male) voyeur, refusing to meet the viewer's gaze. One cannot imagine O'Neill's woman, as opposed to most of Vargas's "girls," standing scantily clad with a wrench in one hand as if to say, "Oh! How did I get here all naked with a wrench in my hand?" O'Neill's woman is a material (if glamorized) reality rather than a mere male fantasy.

Figure 14. The pleasures of popularity

Concluding our first theme, the above sketch (see Fig. 14; also from the 1930s) gives a teenaged vignette, a soon-to-be-common theme of the '50s. Far from mundane, the scene evokes stronger, more complex emotions than a simple day at the soda shop: whereas the first young woman reclines gracefully, displaying the polished, smiling, carefree side of youth, a second woman sits brooding in the background, seemingly neglected and alone. Depicting the first woman's foil or necessary "other," this second shows the more introspective, darker side of a woman's teenaged years.

II. Rose and Callista O'Neill, Suffragettes.

Throughout this second section, we explore themes of feminism and women's suffrage that Rose shared with her younger sister. Though this photograph (see Fig. 15) shows Callista at Bonniebrook, a fuller context is given by Thomas Edgelow, reporter for the 1915 *New York Press*. Invited to the sisters' Washington Square apartments for an interview,

Figure 15. Callista traipsing near Bonniebrook

he describes waiting in their shared drawing room-studio, scanning library shelves: "Shakespeare—Aha! Culture here! They look as if they had been read, too. A volume or two of O'Henry! . . . but Callista O'Neill interrupted just here." Clearly fallen under her spell, Edgelow continues:

> The room suited her in its amber, its black and rose tints, and she suited the room. Very demurely she crossed the floor. "I am Callista O'Neill," she said, and I have come to answer questions until my sister is ready to receive you."
>
> Her name, like her studio, suits her. . . . "It is from the Greek, she explained. My dress, too, had its origin in that source."
>
> She held up her arms so that it could be better seen. It was cut in one piece. The sleeves were elbow length. The general effect was as if she had taken a length of some richly colored material, had cut a hole for the head and had draped Callista in it. The general effect of this garment was Grecian in its simplicity, without a hint at any freakishness.
>
> "Yes," she agreed, "simplicity is the main point, simplicity in making, simplicity in putting it on, simplicity in wearing it. But you must talk to my sister about it all."

Clothing, indeed, was the reason for his visit. Some time in early April 1915, Rose and Callista gave an interview and one-woman "fashion show" to local reporters, speaking in support of a public competition to design new, "polymuriel" clothing for women—a dress that could be worn in all places and occasions (hence the term, "polymuriel") while liberating them from their corsets. In his 25 April 1915 *New York Press* article, titled "Rose O'Neill in Campaign to Introduce Her Novel Art-Garb," Edgelow quotes the artist:

It is quite time that a decisive stroke was struck for freedom of women, not only as regards to the suffrage question, . . . but on other matters. The first step is to free women from the yoke of modern fashions and modern dress. How can they hope to compete with men when they are boxed up tight in the clothes that are worn today?

As Rose held forth on freedom in woman's fashion, Callista "had slipped away and returned in a most beautiful costume." Edgelow continues:

She wore trousers. Yes, trousers. But do not run away with the idea that the dress was masculine or harsh. . . . They were of some soft, silky material and a deep amber color. You have only to look at the drawing Miss O'Neill made to get the idea. Over these Callista wore a kind of Grecian tunic which embodied the grace of olden times with the practicability of to-day.

It is to the following illustration (see Fig. 16) that Edgelow makes reference.

But not all of the city's reporters were as smitten. "Leg Emancipation Women's New Plea," declares the title of an article published in a rival newspaper, the 12 April 1915 *New York Times*. The article's subtitle—"Rose O'Neill Wants Them Free as Her 'Kewpies' at the Waistline and Knees"—hints at the anonymous (and obviously male) staff writer's half-mocking, all-condescending tone:

Rose O'Neill thinks she knows what's the matter with women. Not being a man, and being an artist, Miss O'Neill has a right to think such thoughts, or, at least, she thinks she has.

Miss O'Neill thinks women waste too much energy wearing their clothes. Men might say they wasted too much energy, and time, too, picking their

The "Callista Costume" as worn by Callista O'Neill. —Sketch from life by Rose O'Neill.

Miss Rose O'Neill, of "Kewpies" Fame.

Figure 16. The "Callista Costume," illustrated

clothes and putting them on, but Miss O'Neill now has the floor.

Miss O'Neill says that first women's waists and legs must be released. That's where they use up their energy and their vitality, she says. The force a woman expends bending a corset every time she bends her body, and waggling a skirt each time she moves a leg, could be put to, oh, so much better use, the originator of the "Kewpies" thinks. And, speaking of "Kewpies," Miss O'Neill didn't dress them so that they'd have to waste a lot of energy toting their clothes. She didn't just say she'd dress women up like "Kewpies"; she hadn't time to go into details, she said, but she hinted that the garb of grown females shouldn't be hampering at all if those grown females are to be of the greatest use to the world and themselves.

213

Figure 17. Rose and Callista getting out the vote

Published in the spring of 1915, *The New York Times* article reflected typically masculinist sentiments, none of which boded well for the sisters' feminism. Throughout that year, the City Woman Suffrage Party ran a campaign supporting a city-wide referendum in support of women's voting rights. Ballots were cast on November 2, the CWSP losing in each of New York's boroughs (Jordan 22). Still, the two sisters had done their part. In this photograph (see Fig. 17), Rose (forty-one at the time) stands to the left, facing the camera, while Callista wears her sister's poster in support of the referendum.

And Rose herself was not above tree-stump politicking. As she writes in her autobiography,

> Callista and I were keen about the fight for woman suffrage and I walked in some parades, wore a placard, and made drawings for the cause. One Sunday evening . . . I saw a crowd about a platform. Two of the suffrage workers immediately asked me if I would "hold the crowd" until the next speaker, Will Irwin, arrived. I began well for I was introduced as the mother of the Kewpies to thunderous applause. . . . I was soon aware that the audience was with me . . . [and] when I came down from the platform they received me in their bosoms. As I walked home to Washington Square I felt as if I was walking on air. . . . I kept saying to myself, "I am an orator," and laughing in triumph. (121–23)

In public speaking as in newspaper interviews, Rose's efforts were mixed. Her autobiography continues:

> The next day I was at my drawing-board when two of the suffrage workers came in to ask me if I would return to Madison Square and "hold the crowd" during the noon hour. Full of elation I went. . . . But the people on the benches seemed to be . . . dirty, ragged men, who smelled of alcohol and looked at us with blinking eyes. . . . I tried to awaken them with the arguments I had had such success with the night before . . . . They did not laugh [and] my audience went wearily back to its benches. (123)

"I went back to Washington Square," she adds, "and told myself I was not an orator" (123).

Figure 18. Together for Home and Family

But Rose not only spoke for women's suffrage; she "made drawings for the cause," as previously noted. This poster (see Fig. 18) represents perhaps the finest surviving example of O'Neill's political poster-art: heroic figures both (albeit in modern garb), the man and woman walk side-by-side, suggesting equality. Yet the woman points forward, arm outstretched, leading the way. The poster itself made national news: as noted in *The Los Angeles Tribune*, "The most celebrated of America's black-and-white artists, Rose O'Neill . . . . is an ardent suffragist and an active member of the Press and Publicity Council of New York City. To aid in their campaign for 'Votes for Women Nov 2,' she has just designed and donated to them the striking poster here reproduced" (NWHP). Originally printed for the New York City elections of 2 November 1915, the poster was reused in 1917, when a similar referendum was placed on the November 6 ballot (hence the "correction" from 2 to 6)—this second time successfully.

III. On Sisterhood: Rose and Callista, Together.

While sorority remained foundational to the women's suffrage movement, the offices of sisterhood were, for Rose O'Neill, more than ideology or abstractions. Unwavering and fiercely loyal, Rose lived her life in deep concord with the "'little sister' of the O'Neill family of Bonniebrook, inseparable companion and secretary to her famous sister": so reads Callista O'Neill's obituary, from the 16 October 1946 *Kansas City (MO) Times*. By age twenty-one, Callista had become her sister's sidekick-secretary. And though she might stray occasionally from her older sister's side, Callista would always come back: her marriage (soon after World War I) to Eric Schuler lasted four years and, likely, was doomed from the start. As a rival for the younger sister's attention, Schuler (d. 1937) simply could not compete with Rose.

This is not to suggest that Callista consciously "chose" her sister over marriage: the siblings' soul-mate intimacy was not unusual for the time. And it would be unfair to cast Callista as a mere "junior partner" in their relationship, since she was herself an accomplished artist, Rose's equal in charm, and a major influence upon her more famous sister's art: she became, as it were, Rose's living model for creative, free-spirited, sensuous, unfettered womanhood. For this reason, one cannot separate Callista from Rose's mature artistry.

Though identifying with one another, they were not identical: that is, their bonds did not reduce them to mere shadows of their sibling "other." Bearing witness to this paradox, Horine (29) records two anecdotes by Calcuttan poet, Dahn Gopal Mukerji, the first that "Rose and Callista were two beaks from the same bird," the second that "Rose had drunk the sun but Callista had spilled the moon." This latter, Horine adds, "was a perfect comparison of the sisters, both in manner and dress. While Rose usually wore rose or wine colored velvet mantles over peach colored silk gowns, Callista . . . complimented [sic] the red Rose by wearing pale shades of blue or green of the Grecian style" (20). In each, the other found her complement.

We have already discussed a photograph of Callista "traipsing" near Bonniebrook, which hints at her communion with Nature—a practice that, nowadays, might be derided as "tree-hugging," though previous generations treated "Mother Nature" as a creative muse in itself. (And what better place for the sisters to regain creative energy than the Ozarks, with its pristine beauty?) In fact, it belongs to a sequence of photographs showing Rose's sister dancing in the manner of another contemporary iconoclast, Isadora Duncan (see Fig. 19). Dance was, apparently, one of Callista's passions, as Edgelow, *The New York Press* reporter, describes in his previously-cited article: back in the sisters' Washington

Square apartments, after she had donned Rose's "novel art-garb,"

> a gramophone was brought in and set a-working and Callista danced. It would be impossible to describe how her costume lent itself in all beauty to the dance. She was the incarnation of Spring itself.
>
> Callista has often been begged by a multitude of her artistic friends to dance in public. If she does, New York will open its eyes.
>
> "I may do so yet," she confided, "but if I do, it will be for the cause of suffrage. I shall dance a little, and if the people are pleased I shall talk a little to them about women."

For Callista, it would seem that the free-flowing movement of modern dance expressed—or, perhaps better, released—the *jouissance* of womanhood.

Figure 19. Callista at Bonniebrook, dancing

Figure 20. Callista, seductress

Though "dainty and fairy-like" (Horine 29) in the eyes of some, Callista grew in her sister's artistic imagination, especially given the younger sibling's grace and strength of movement. Boldly stylized, the above sketch (see Fig. 20) depicts Roses's sister in an entrancing, Salome-like dance: her piercing, forward-staring eyes and powerful arm-swing seem to cast their glamour over spectators.

IV. Toward a Conclusion.

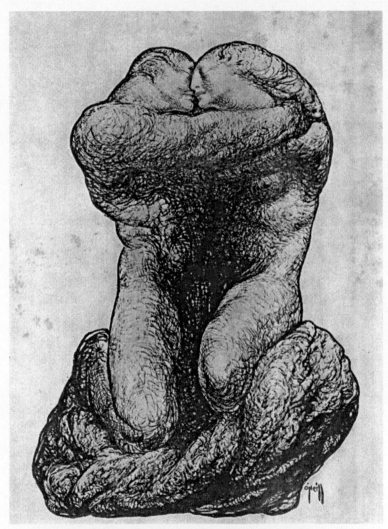

Figure 21. O'Neill's "Master-Mistress"

More, obviously, can be said of Rose's art, her sexuality, her psychology. In "Four Poems to Kallista," a sequence from her well-received lyric collection, *The Master-Mistress* (1922), Rose elaborates on the intimacies of sisterhood, seemingly addressing Callista directly: "I put you on as silk attire," she writes, and "don you as a garment." Elsewhere, she "make[s] a banquet" of Callista, consuming her as "bread" and "wine." Indeed, Rose's understanding of love rests in the "holy" mysteries of communion, of two made one flesh. An illustration from *The Master-Mistress* (see Fig. 21), the "monster" drawing shows two chthonic lovers intertwined, hewn from the self-same rock (and hinting, thus, at an hermaphroditic union of opposites).

Previously mentioned, her "sweet monster" drawings (which formed the core of her 1920s New York and Paris exhibitions) deserve an essay in themselves, as do Rose's poems, both collected and unpublished. A consideration of these materials—which stand at the apex of Rose's mature artistry, both visual and literary—would surely complicate the analysis given thus far; but such an essay belongs to a future volume of *Moon City Review.* As the present essay demonstrates, Rose Cecil O'Neill's artwork charted the changing cultural landscape of "modern" American women, and did so from the viewpoint of a woman artist who not only lived through those changes, but helped bring them about.

Works Cited

"Callista O'Neill Dies." *The Kansas City (MO) Times*, 16 October 1946. N.p. (clipping from The David O'Neill Collection).

Edgelow, Thomas. "Rose O'Neill in Campaign to Introduce her Novel Art-Garb." *The New York Press*, 25 April 1915. 5:1.

"Fair Tresses Are 'Bobbed.'" *The Washington Post*, 26 March 1916. 1:14.

Formanek-Brunell, Miriam. *The Story of Rose O'Neill: An Autobiography.* Columbia: U of Missouri P, 1997.

Horine, Maude M. *Memories of Rose O'Neill.* Branson MO: Persimmon Patch, 1950.

Jordan, Vernon D., Jr. *Around the Korner: Women's Suffrage and Rose O'Neill.* Des Moines, IA: Wings, 2009.

King, Alexander. "PROFILES: Kewpie Doll." *The New Yorker*, 24 November 1934. N.p. Facs. rpt. in *Rose O'Neill Scrapbook.* Ed. Francis J. Gibbons and Robert H. Gibbons. Springfield MO: Bonniebrook Enterprises, 1971. N.p.

"Leg Emancipation Women's New Plea." *The New York Times*, 12 April 1915. 2:6.

McCanse, Ralph Alan. *Titans and Kewpies: The Life and Art of Rose O'Neill.* New York: Vantage, 1968.

"Mystical and Humorous." Review of *The Loves of Edwy. The New York Times*, 10 September 1905. 2:27.

NWHP: National Women's History Project, Women's History Month. *2008 Honoree: Rose O'Neill.* 1 July 2009. <http://www.nwhp.org/whm/oneill_bio.php>.

O'Neill, Rose Cecil. *The Loves of Edwy.* Boston: Lothrop, 1904.

———. *The Master-Mistress: Poems, with Drawings by the Author.* New York: Alfred A. Knopf, 1922.

"Rose O'Neill Dies." *Springfield (MO) Leader and Press*, 6 April 1944. N.p. (clipping from The David O'Neill Collection).

Ruggles, Rowena Godding. *The One Rose: A Biography of Rose O'Neill and the Story of Her Work*. 2nd ed. Albany, CA: n.p., 1972.

Vreeland, Diana. *D.V.* Ed. George Plimpton and Christopher Hemphill. New York: Random House/Vintage, 1984.

"Women Who Lead the Way." *The New York Times*, 20 February 1921. 7:1.

"Would Save the Ozarks." *The Des Moines News*, 26 December 1916. 1:4.

Illustrations and Credits

Again, we thank David O'Neill for permission to reproduce the above materials, all of which came from his collection. Unless otherwise noted, images were reproduced digitally by staff at the Meyer Library Special Collections and Archives, Missouri State University.

Figure 1. "Rose reclining at Bonniebrook." Photograph © David O'Neill.

Figure 2. "Kewpies marching for woman's suffrage, 1915." Postcard © David O'Neill, digital reproduction by Vernon D. Jordan, Jr.

Figure 3. "Rose painting at Caradossi's Studio, Paris." Photograph © David O'Neill.

Figure 4. "Rose at work in Bonniebrook." Photograph © David O'Neill.

Figure 5. "A study in self-portraiture." Pencil drawing © David O'Neill.

Figure 6. "A studio portrait of Rose, ca. 1904." Photograph © David O'Neill.

Notes on Contributors

CAROL AUTERSON is a graduate student in the Missouri State Theater and Dance Department.

JAMES S. BAUMLIN teaches English at Missouri State. He has published widely in fields of criticism, the history of rhetoric, and English renaissance poetry.

JULIE BLACKMON won the *American Photo's* Emerging Photographer award in 2008, and has exhibited her work nationally and internationally. Her published work includes the volume of photography, *Domestic Vacations.*

KEVIN BROCKMEIER is the author of the novels *The Brief History of the Dead* and *The Truth About Celia*, the story collections *Things That Fall from the Sky* and *The View from the Seventh Layer*, and the children's novels *City of Names* and *Grooves: A Kind of Mystery.* He earned a BA in English from Missouri State.

DAKOTAH BURNS, formerly of Springfield, Missouri, lives in Louisville, Kentucky and studies English at the University of Louisville.

MICHAEL BURNS is Emeritus Professor of English at Missouri State, where he taught creative writing. A graduate of the creative writing program at the University of Arkansas, Fayetteville, he has published several poetry collections, including *The Secret Names* and *It Will Be All Right in the Morning.*

SHANNON BURNS earned a BA in English from The University of Louisville, where she is now a law student. Her chapbook, *Preserving the Old Way of Life,* is available from Factory Hollow Press.

LEE BUSBY received his MA at Missouri State University and is currently pursuing his MFA at Vermont College of Fine Arts.

LANETTE CADLE is an Assistant Professor of English at Missouri State. She is Senior Editor for *Computers and Composition Online* and her poems have appeared in *Crab Orchard Review.* She is also a recipient of the Merton Poetry of the Sacred Award.

MARCUS CAFAGÑA is the author of two books of poetry, *The Broken World* and *Roman Fever.* His poems have also appeared in *Ploughshares, Poetry,*

226

and *The Southern Review*. He coordinates the creative writing program at Missouri State.

BILLY CLEM is a doctoral candidate in English and Creative Writing at Northern Illinois University and Associate Professor of English at Waubonsee Community College. He has published work in *Lodestar Quarterly* and *Elder Mountain*.

MICHAEL CZYZNIEJEWSKI grew up in Chicago and now lives in Ohio, where he teaches at Bowling Green State University and serves as Editor-in-Chief of *Mid-American Review*. Recent stories have recently appeared or are forthcoming in *Alaska Quarterly Review, Bellingham Review, Monkeybicycle,* and *The Los Angeles Review*. His debut collection, *Elephants in Our Bedroom*, was released in early 2009 from Dzanc Books.

JOHN DUFRESNE is the author of two collections of stories and four novels, most recently *Requiem, Mass*. He teaches creative writing at Florida International University in Miami.

PAIGE FREESEMAN received her BFA in Ceramics from Kansas State University. She is currently a MA student in Art Therapy at Nazareth University in Rochester, New York.

D. GILSON is a graduate student in creative writing and teaching assistant at Missouri State.

WARREN HAYS graduated in 2009 with a BA in Creative Writing from Missouri State.

CHRIS HELMS earned an MA in English from Missouri State in 2008 and currently lives in Fayetteville, Arkansas.

JAKE HELTON is a graduate student in creative writing and teaching assistant at Missouri State.

David Hill is an Electronic Arts major and a Creative Writing minor at Missouri State.

SAMUEL HITCHCOCK earned his BFA in Art from Missouri State. His work is carried by Mobilia Gallery, Cambridge, Massachusetts.

JANE HOOGESTRAAT is Professor of English at Missouri State. Her chapbook *Harvesting All Night* won the Finishing Line Press 2008 Competition.

ARTHUR HUBER graduated from USC with a degree in English, currently teaches in Korea, and plans to attend graduate school this coming fall at the University of Colorado in Boulder. This is his first published poem.

TED KOOSER served two terms as U.S. Poet Laureate, and during his second term won the Pulitzer Prize for Poetry.

NATHAN MASTERS lives in Illinois. This is his first published poem.

JEREMIAH MOORHEAD received his BA in English Literature from Missouri State in 2006. He currently works as a caseworker to the homeless in Springfield, MO, where he lives with his wife and 15 month-old son.

BEN PFEIFFER received his BS in Cinematography and Film Editing from Missouri State University. He is currently finishing his first novel and pursuing his MFA in Fiction at the University of Kansas.

BURTON RAFFEL writes, "Translation is an art, but a secondary one. Though his publishing record does not show it, Burton Raffel has always focused most intently on his poetry and fiction." As an editor and translator, he has published more than one hundred books.

LAURA REGER is a BSEd English major and a Spanish minor at Missouri State.

BILL SHULTZ earned a BA in Creative Writing from Missouri State in 2008.

JENNIFER SMITH earned an MA in English from Missouri State and currently lives near Pittsburgh.

APRIL STUBLEFIELD graduated from Missouri State in 2009 and is currently in the School Counseling Masters Program there.

LIAM R. WATTS is a graduate student earning his MA at Missouri State.

ASHLEY WATSON is a senior Psychology major at Missouri State.

SATARAH WHEELER is originally from Reeds Spring, Missouri, and is currently a senior Creative Writing major at Missouri State University.

MILLER WILLIAMS is Emeritus Professor of English at the University of Arkansas, Fayetteville, and was the first director of the University of Arkansas Press. In 1997, he read a poem at President Clinton's inauguration. His numerous book publications include *Some Jazz Awhile: Collected Poems* and *Making a Poem: Some Thoughts About Poetry and the People Who Write It*.

SHANNON WOODEN is both an alumna and faculty member at Missouri State University. Her PhD in Victorian Literature is from the University of North Carolina, where she also served as fiction editor of the *Carolina Quarterly*. She has published articles on literary representations of science, medicine, race, and gender, as well as on pop culture and contemporary fiction.

MEAGHAN YOUNKER earned her BA in Communication from Missouri State and is currently a graduate student in Communication.

Moon City Press is a joint venture of the Missouri State University
Departments of English and Art and Design.
With series lists in "Arts and Letters" and
"Ozarks History and Culture,"
Moon City Press
features collaborations
between students and faculty
over the various aspects of publication:
research, writing, editing, layout and design.

LaVergne, TN USA
12 October 2009

160588LV00003B/3/P